SON OF MAN

JOHN DRANE

SON OF MAN

A *new life of Christ*

Photography by
Sonia Halliday Photographs

William B. Eerdmans Publishing Company
Grand Rapids, Michigan

For Len and Lesley

ACKNOWLEDGMENTS

All photographs are by Sonia Halliday Photographs:
F.H.C. Birch p.12;
Sonia Halliday p.9, 15 top, 16, 19, 26, 30, 35, 37, 39, 44, 47,
    62, 65 top, 70, 79, 84, 87, 88, 95, 99, 107 top, 115, 117,
    119, 121, 122/3, 132, 133, 139, 145, 148, 152, 155;
Sonia Halliday & Laura Lushington p. 43 top, 52, 55 top, 76,
    112, 146, 149;
Barry Searle p.10, 18, 28, 49, 69, 73, 75, 80, 101;
Jane Taylor p.20, 32, 40, 43 below left, below right, 55 below,
    57, 60, 83, 93, 97, 104, 107 below, 111, 113, 116;
Barbara Warley p.81.

Illustrations p. 130, 156-7 by Tony Dover.

Maps and diagrams by Tony Cantale Graphics.

Acknowledgment is also due to G. Vermes, for the extract
used on p.147 from *Jesus the Jew* (London: Collins 1973),
p.41, and to R. Bultmann for the quotation used on p.154
from *The Theology of the Old Testament*, Vol 1 (London:
SCM Press 1952), p.176.

CONTENTS

Preface

There was probably never a period in my life when I didn't know who Jesus was. But I remember very clearly the first time I began to take him seriously. It was the result of a religious education class in high school, and my interest was sparked off by the arrival of a new and inexperienced teacher who was having difficulty controlling the class. As one of the leading troublemakers in that group, I remember telling him that none of us believed, or even took seriously, anything to do with religion – for we all knew that the rationalist, materialist mindset of the European Enlightenment had made belief impossible for thinking people. I didn't put it quite like that at the time, for I had never heard of the Enlightenment then. But it had a profound impact on the way that kids of the 1960s were thinking. I shall never forget the teacher's response: he simply asked me if I'd ever read the Bible, or indeed anything else to do with religion. I knew the answer, but was reluctant to admit it and look foolish. But I left class that day determined that by the next time I met him, I would indeed have read something, and be in a position to ask more informed, and, I supposed, more provocative, questions.

I went home that night, took a Bible and began to read the stories of Jesus. I chose Mark's gospel, because I reckoned that was the shortest account of his life and teaching. I was hardly prepared for the sense of surprise and discovery which accosted me. I was surprised because I discovered it was actually possible to read a book of the Bible the same way as any other book – by starting at the beginning and reading to the end. That might seem an obvious thing, but none of the Christians I knew would ever have dreamed of doing it: they generally restricted their Bible reading to a couple of sentences at any one time, as if it was so hard to comprehend it needed a long time to chew over even a short section. I was even more surprised when it turned out to be quite an interesting story. Indeed, I soon realized that the common stereotypes of this Jesus were not exactly accurate. He was not a saint imprisoned in a stained glass window, too good to be true. Nor was he a theological dogma, too complex to understand. On the contrary, he seemed to be an ordinary person relating to other ordinary people, who, give or take the odd detail, were people like me. Not quite, because with Jesus these ordinary people – fishermen, tax collectors, prostitutes, thieves — seemed empowered to do extraordinary things. Things like changing the course of world history — things that appealed to me when we were all struggling to make sense of the inhumanities of Vietnam, constantly wondering what horrors the world superpowers would unleash on us, and all the time knowing that we had the power to make the future what we wanted it to be.

Like many others of my generation, I became fascinated by this enigmatic figure who, unlike the religious establishment we knew, seemed to share our idealism, and inspire ordinary people to great things. During the intervening years, I have read and re-read the stories of Jesus many times, but I have never lost that sense of new discovery and excitement. Jesus remains as compelling as ever, and just as challenging. My own understanding of him has developed, and I am conscious of the fact that what follows is very much a personal portrait of Jesus. A major influence is my awareness of the fact that today, most of Jesus' followers no longer live in the "Christian west". People like me are in a minority among the world's Christians, more than 60 per cent of whom are non-white, non-western, and whose numbers are growing all the time. In recent years I have been enormously privileged to meet with Christians on every continent, and to share in the vibrant discoveries they are making about Jesus and his message. The Bible looks different when viewed from the perspective of the poor, the oppressed and the exploited.

Arguably, such people have a more authentic understanding.

At any rate, their understandings have enriched me in far-reaching ways: while traditional western Christianity has generally imprisoned Jesus in the straitjacket of what happens in church buildings on Sunday mornings, these people have taken his teaching at face value, and applied it to the whole of life. This has gone hand-in-hand with new ways of reading the New Testament texts, and many western scholars can now see the value of asking sociological and psychological questions born of our own experience of life, even if they still persist with the historical and literary concerns of our rationalist predecessors.

New questions force us to look for new answers. As we come to the end of a century that has seen more violence than almost any other in the whole of human history, we need new perspectives on old traditions, new understandings of ourselves and our place in the cosmic order of things, and new directions for the future. In this context, I make no apology for producing yet another "life of Christ". I only seek to share what I have myself learned, while recognizing that all our discoveries are provisional. If you are happy to join me on this pilgrimage of exploration, and if it all makes sense as we approach the start of the third millennium, then that will be sufficient justification for yet another book on this ancient yet ever-present character, the "Son of Man".

John Drane.

AUGUST 1993

IN THE BEGINNING

1

SETTING THE SCENE

THE STORY of Jesus of Nazareth is one of the most enduring and fascinating of all time. He has an aura of mystique and charm that are hard to beat. He has never had an advertising manager, yet for decades the stories of his life have featured among the world's best-sellers, and the Bible has been translated into more languages than any other book. His intrinsic fascination is so compelling that people from all cultures and every continent find themselves naturally drawn to him. He lived almost 2000 years ago, yet today he is worshipped as divine by millions of people around the world.

Christians are not the only ones who find themselves charmed by him. His admirers can as easily be found among devout Muslims and Hindus, as well as western spiritual searchers attracted by the New Age Movement. Even those who cannot accept his grandiose claims about his own ultimate significance still frequently find themselves trying to model their lives on his ethical teaching.

Bedouin shepherd watches over his flock of sheep and goats.

Commitment to Jesus Christ has led people to the most incredible acts of selfless love. It has also led to some of the most unspeakably horrific acts of violence the world has ever seen.

This one unique individual has had such a profound impact not only in his own day, but on the whole history of civilisation, that we can scarcely underestimate his importance. But what is the truth about Jesus? What was he really like? What was his teaching? And what was he asking of the rest of us? Can we trust what the Bible says about him? And even if we can, how can we begin to assess it all for ourselves?

These questions – and others like them – will all be tackled somewhere in this book. But first, we must start at the very beginning : the familiar stories of the first Christmas, in which the New Testament writers tell of the birth of this remarkable person.

NATIVITY

We all have our mental images of what it must have been like. Mostly gleaned from Christmas cards and church nativity plays.

THE WORLD OF JESUS

To understand Jesus fully, we need to get him into proper perspective. Like the rest of us, he belongs in a particular time and place. First-century Palestine, on the eastern fringe of the ancient Roman empire. And much of his teaching and behaviour only comes to life when we set him in that context.

His world was radically different from ours. Nowadays, anyone can easily travel to the other side of the globe in a matter of little more than 24 hours. But Jesus never moved more than about 80-100 kilometres from his home town. Even if we choose to stay at home, we can move around our towns and cities quite easily. But Jesus had never seen even a bicycle, let alone a car or public

transportation system. We can admire the beauty of the world which is our home from photographs taken from satellites circling hundreds of miles above the atmosphere. Jesus' contemporaries thought of the world as a giant cake with three layers – the realm of the dead under the ground, the flat earth in the middle, and heaven up above. If we could be taken back in a magical time machine, we would suffer more than just culture shock: it would be like life on a different planet altogether.

Not quite. For some things never seem to change much at all. And in the world that Jesus knew, political influence and military power were no less highly prized than they are now. Not that there was a great deal of

noticeable tension in the world at large. In fact, the world government at the time was remarkably stable. But that was only because the military might of the Roman empire had established itself so firmly in power, and with such brutality, that very few people cared to question its authority. In any case, most of its inhabitants enjoyed a reasonable standard of living, and could look to it for protection and justice.

The Romans did not so much create their empire, as inherit it. For the basic shape of the Roman world was settled long before the time of Jesus, by the Greek genius Alexander the Great. A native of Macedon in northern Greece, this young general set out to conquer the world in 323 BC. Ten years later, he had done it. With an empire stretching from Greece to what is modern Pakistan,

Snowy streets, romantic angelic choirs, a stable full of animated cows and horses, perhaps a robin or two, some shepherds watching their flocks on a Palestinian hillside – they are all an indispensable part of the modern Christmas. Not forgetting the child himself, of course, nestled comfortably in a stoutly made manger filled with crisp, golden straw, while the proud parents, Joseph and Mary, look on – simply clad, though with every appearance of having stepped straight from the local Palestinian boutique.

If that's your image of what really happened, then forget it. The birth of Jesus was probably nothing like that at all. For one thing, it is highly unlikely that there was any snow around at the time. It does snow on the Judean hills, but shepherds would never stay

Alexander the Great, from the mosaic celebrating victory over the Persians at Issus. He shaped the political map that the Romans eventually inherited.

Greek political structures would be adopted in cities everywhere. And Greek gods and goddesses were to be worshipped in temples originally constructed to honour other deities.

Alexander never lived to see his grand vision come to fruition. He died at the age of 33, mysteriously struck down by disease on the borders of India. In political terms, his empire died with him. His realm was divided among his four generals, none of whom enjoyed his personal charisma or popularity. But his vision lived on. The Greek way of life was enthusiastically adopted by people of other races, and a unity of purpose was established throughout the Mediterranean world that made it very easy for the Roman general Octavian (63 BC – AD 14) eventually to reunite Alexander's domain and create out of it the beginnings of the

he was to set the pace for life throughout the region for the next thousand years or more.

Though his conquests were achieved by military might, Alexander was by nature a conciliatory person, and he allowed a good deal of autonomy to vanquished nations. But there was one thing that motivated him above everything else. He was absolutely convinced that his own native Greek culture was the very best in the world. In fact, he thought it was the most sophisticated culture there had ever been – or was ever likely to be. For him, Greek literature, philosophy, politics and religion represented the very pinnacle of human achievement. A perfect way of life. So wherever he went he set up a vigorous programme to share all things Greek with those whom he met. The Greek language was destined to become the official language of the whole of his empire.

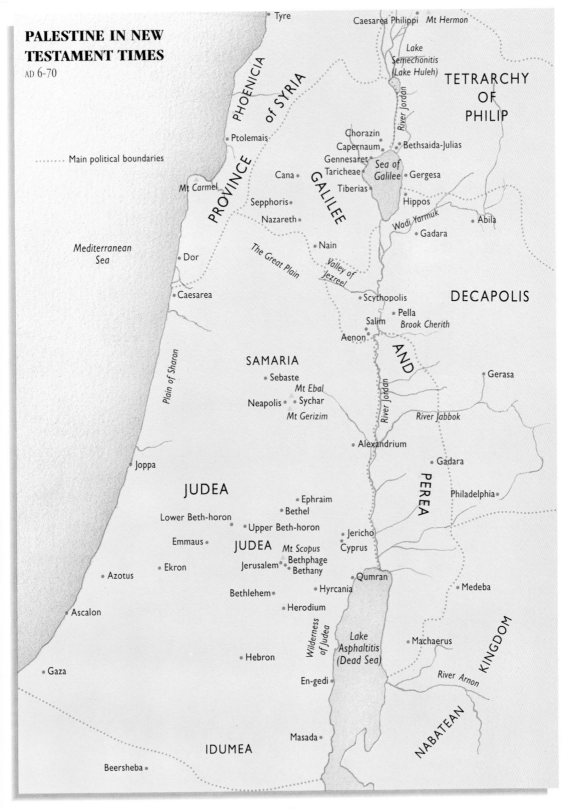

PALESTINE IN NEW TESTAMENT TIMES

AD 6-70

Tyre

Caesarea Philippi · Mt Hermon

Lake Semechonitis (Lake Huleh)

TETRARCHY OF PHILIP

PHOENICIA

PROVINCE of SYRIA

· Ptolemais

Chorazin ·

Capernaum · · Bethsaida-Julias

Gennesaret ·

Taricheae · Sea of Galilee · Gergesa

· Cana

GALILEE

Tiberias ·

· Mt Carmel

Hippos ·

· Sepphoris

· Abila

· Nazareth

Wadi Yarmuk

· Gadara

········ Main political boundaries

· Nain

The Great Plain

Valley of Jezreel

River Jordan

Mediterranean Sea

· Dor

Scythopolis ·

DECAPOLIS

· Caesarea

· Pella

Salim · Brook Cherith

Aenon ·

Plain of Sharon

AND

SAMARIA

· Sebaste

· Gerasa

Mt Ebal

Neapolis · · Sychar

Mt Gerizim

River Jordan

River Jabbok

· Alexandrium

PEREA

· Joppa

· Gadara

JUDEA

· Ephraim

· Bethel

· Philadelphia

Lower Beth-horon ·

· Upper Beth-horon

· Jericho

Emmaus ·

JUDEA

Mt Scopus

· Cyprus

Jerusalem · · Bethphage

· Ekron

· Bethany

· Qumran

· Azotus

· Medeba

Bethlehem ·

· Hyrcania

NABATEAN KINGDOM

· Ascalon

· Herodium

Wilderness of Judea

Lake Asphaltitis (Dead Sea)

· Machaerus

· Hebron

· Gaza

River Arnon

En-gedi ·

· Masada

IDUMEA

· Beersheba

out all night in those conditions. The fact that they were watching their flocks in the open air suggests Jesus was born at almost any time of year except winter. So people who celebrate Christmas today in the heat of the southern hemisphere are probably nearer the original conditions than those from the frozen north.

Nor would the stable be a particularly congenial place in which to give birth. Even the most ardent advocate of natural childbirth would find little to emulate here – especially for the birth of a mother's first child. And it is certainly unlikely to have been witnessed by regimented rows of awe-struck beasts resting in squeaky-clean straw. The real Christmas was rather different.

It began not in the stable – nor even in Bethlehem – but back in a small village called Nazareth. A nondescript place something like 180 kilometres distant from Bethlehem, Nazareth was of no real consequence in the power politics of the day. Indeed, to come from Nazareth was a mark of social inferiority to many. When the strict Jewish believer Nathanael heard of Jesus' origins there and asked whimsically, "Can anything good come from

Roman empire, that would last for another five hundred years or so.

This was the world into which Jesus was born. A world that in name was dominated by the Romans, but whose basic culture was Greek. In Palestine – as elsewhere – Greek was the official language, and no doubt Jesus would be familiar with it. But in Palestine, there had always been an uneasy tension between this Greek culture – Hellenism as it was called – and the native culture of the Jewish people. Every other nation of the Mediterranean world had adopted a pragmatic attitude to the programme of enforced Hellenisation instigated by Alexander's successors. Of course, it meant a certain loss of national sovereignty. But no one – certainly not Alexander – ever insisted that conquered races should actually give up their own way of life. They were allowed to retain their own native languages, customs and religion – just so long as they adopted Greek ways alongside them. For most, this was no problem. If it meant the Greek god Zeus had to stand with the ancient gods of Egypt or Syria, that was no particular complication. Indeed, many people regarded the addition of more gods to the local temples as a dynamic new way to enhance the original splendour and spiritual power of such places.

But for Jews, it was not quite so simple. They only had one God to start with – and this God was not traditionally worshipped with the aid of idols or statues. More than that, the Hebrew Bible actually forbade the use of such visual representations – a prohibition that was frequently understood to extend to any form of artistic endeavour, including the painting and sculpture that were so central to the Greek way of life. Not that these strictures had always been carefully observed in practice. Archaeologists have discovered many religious figurines dating back a thousand years before the time of Christ, some of them depicting female forms, and all clearly used in Israelite worship. Five hundred years later, Jews in the temple of Elephantine in Egypt were still following the same practices – while the books of the Old Testament prophets show clearly enough that, whatever the ideals might have been, in reality much popular worship was quite different. By the time of Alexander, however, the Jewish nation had been through a time of great upheaval and crisis. The Babylonian tyrant, Nebuchadnezzar II, had destroyed Jerusalem –

Nazareth?", he was no doubt voicing the cynical attitudes of many strict Jews. In fact, so little is known of Nazareth that a couple of generations ago sceptical historians actually doubted whether there was such a place at all in the lifetime of Jesus! Nazareth was in Galilee, and the whole of this territory was of little consequence to the inhabitants of the main Jewish centres in Judea. For one thing, it was rather small, and the whole of Galilee could be fitted into the English county of Wiltshire or the Grand Duchy of Luxembourg. For another, it had rather a large Gentile population, and was often thought too open to non-Jewish cultural influences. But there can be no doubt this was

Many scrolls of Old Testament scriptures were found hidden in jars in caves at Qumran, by the Dead Sea.

THE ROMAN EMPIRE
Early first century AD

page 15

including its famous temple – and deported most of its leading citizens off into forced exile in Mesopotamia. As a result, the nation lost its heart, and inevitably began a period of extensive self-examination to try and understand what had happened. The answer seemed almost self-evident: compromise with other cultures and religions had led to personal calamity and national disintegration on a grand scale. As new leaders emerged in this so-called post-exilic age, their message was clear: such a thing must never be allowed to happen again. So when people like Ezra demanded that Jews who were involved in marriage with people of other races should divorce their Gentile partners, there was no

shortage of zealous nationalists who were prepared to do just that. What was adopted as a code for personal life was promoted as the ideal for the life of the nation too. So when one of Alexander's successors decreed that Greek ways of life and belief should be officially enforced in Palestine, it was inevitable that it would lead to conflict. The storm broke in a big way when the Greek ruler Antiochus IV (175-164 BC) insisted that altars to Zeus should be built in every village throughout the land, and that pigs (unclean animals to the Jews) be sacrificed on them.

Antiochus not only looted the temple treasury. He also took away some of the people of Jerusalem into slavery, and banned circumcision,

An Arab crosses an old courtyard in Bethlehem.

sabbath observance, and reading the Jewish Law – all things very dear to the hearts of loyal Jewish worshippers. To add insult to injury, he arranged for Zeus to be worshipped in the Jerusalem temple itself, and allowed anyone who wished – Jews or not – to worship there. To back up these uncompromising demands, Antiochus utilised some unspeakably cruel methods. On one occasion, his soldiers constructed huge frying pans in which they cooked alive entire families of people who refused to accept any compromise with their ancestral faith. Yet, brutal and where Jesus grew up: all the gospels report that he had his home in Nazareth as a child, and Joseph and Mary lived there before his birth.

At the time Mary, the mother of Jesus, was in the process of getting married to Joseph. This was an extended business, and it could take several months, with various betrothal ceremonies to get through before the couple were actually pronounced wife and husband. The fact that Mary discovered she was pregnant before the marriage formalities were completed naturally caused Joseph some distress and embarrassment. Both of them would be teenagers at the time.

Today, the events surrounding the conception of Mary's remarkable child are celebrated in the stunning architecture of the Church of the Annunciation in Nazareth: a gleaming modern sanctuary, completed in 1969 but incorporating the remains of earlier churches on the same site. Local tradition also connects a spring on the north side of Nazareth with the angel's announcement to Mary, and pictures her at the Virgin's Fountain,

determined though he was, Antiochus learned his lesson the hard way. Within an amazingly short space of time, his well-disciplined forces were defeated by guerilla fighters organised by just one family (the Maccabees), who restored what they saw as spiritual purity to the Jerusalem temple. The struggle began in 167 BC, and by December 164 BC, his policies had been reversed.

As custodians of the renewed temple, the descendants of the Maccabees also gained considerable political power, and in no time at all had established themselves as a dynasty of priest-kings in the province: the Hasmoneans. Many Jews heralded their accession as the start of a new golden age, in which their ancient heritage would once more be respected, and people of

Jewish birth would hold the reins of power. But it was not to be. The Hasmoneans turned out to be at least as corrupt as their Hellenistic predecessors, and presented the same religious challenges to those who wished to remain firmly committed to the Old Testament heritage. There was much turmoil in the land at this time, as various reactionary sects manoeuvred for position. During this period, the monastic community of Essenes at Qumran was established. These people believed themselves to be the true heirs and successors to the legitimate priesthood, but since they were powerless to do anything about it they withdrew into the Judean desert, there to await some future divine intervention which, they believed, would give them the opportunity to restore the temple and its worship to its original simple

purity. Once in the desert, they established a highly structured religious community, and it was here that the Dead Sea Scrolls were compiled.

Others were just as unhappy with the way things were going, but saw no future for themselves in total withdrawal from mainstream religious life. The Pharisees probably emerged as one such group, and continued to function most effectively as a reform group within mainstream Judaism. No doubt some of these people had political aspirations of their own. But all that was overtaken with the arrival of the Romans on the soil of Palestine.

in conversation with the angel whose name is preserved in the church of St Gabriel. The New Testament says nothing about the place or circumstances in which either Mary or Joseph received the momentous news that Jesus was to be the first child in their family. But it does emphasise that both of them independently received divine confirmation of the fact. In Joseph's case, the gospels record that "an angel of the Lord appeared to him in a dream" (Matthew 1:20), though no mention is made of the precise way in which Mary met the angel Gabriel (Luke 1:26-38). To the New Testament writers, the exact nature of such experiences was not the most important detail. What was crucial, however, was that the birth of Jesus was announced long before it took place, and that Mary and Joseph both knew from the outset that their son was to be very special. Indeed, more than merely

The holy family fled to Egypt to avoid destruction from the hand of King Herod. The Giza pyramids.

special. In the exalted language of Luke's story, "He will be great and will be called the Son of the Most High God ... he will be the king ... his kingdom will never end".

ROMANS AND HERODS

When the Roman general Pompey entered Jerusalem in 63 BC after a siege lasting more than two months, it was the beginning of one of the most turbulent periods in the whole of Jewish history. Pompey was aware of the religious sensitivities of the Jewish people, though one of his first acts on entering Jerusalem was to march straight into the Holy of Holies in the temple – a specially sacred spot where only the high priest was allowed to tread, and then only once a year.

The nation was already torn apart by its own internal tensions. Two factions of the Hasmonean dynasty, headed up by rivals Hyrcanus and Aristobulus, had been locked in a power struggle for some time, and Pompey was inevitably forced to take sides. So far as the Romans were concerned, Hyrcanus had been the more co-operative of the two, and was rewarded by being made high priest and president of the nation, while Aristobulus and his family were taken away to Rome to become a public spectacle as part of Pompey's victory parade.

Pompey's major concern, however, was to establish good Roman administration throughout the whole of Syria and Palestine. To accomplish this, he divided the Jewish state into its natural districts: Judea, Samaria, Galilee and Perea. In addition, various independent Greek cities previously annexed by Hasmonean kings were united in a new coalition to form the Roman province of Syria. Pompey also founded the Decapolis at this time – a group of ten cities (later to become

fourteen), all but one of which were on the eastern side of the river Jordan.

Within less than ten years, however, the country was once more pushed to the verge of anarchy. The exiled Aristobulus managed to escape from Rome and get back to Palestine, where he became the focus of yet more unrest. Aulus Gabinius, proconsul of Syria, was forced to sub-divide Judea into five smaller districts, in order to try and divide the opposition. The five cities of Jerusalem, Gadara, Amathus, Jericho, and Sepphoris, all became

administrative centres of a district. It was a system which worked well, and continued with little change throughout the whole period of Roman rule. But that did not immediately guarantee peace and stability in the region. This time the cause of turmoil was the victory of Julius Caesar, who in 48 BC disposed of Pompey and took over the empire himself. Antipater, a Jewish opportunist connected to the Hasmonean family, ingratiated himself with Caesar, and in return

An altar for burnt offerings in the sanctuary of the temple at Tel Arad, date around the ninth century BC

was made a Roman citizen and procurator of Judea.

If there was one thing the Romans could never tolerate, it was instability. They were far-sighted enough to realise that the imposition of any sort of direct Roman rule in Palestine would always be resisted. It would be bound to arouse the same sort of fanatical opposition that had been the undoing of Antiochus. At the same time, Palestine was a key part of their empire. It effectively marked their eastern boundary, and for that reason it was doubly important to have strong control over it. The Romans knew that they had a desperate need for just one thing: a trustworthy Jewish family to rule on their behalf. Antipater and his family seemed the ideal choice.

Under Antipater's direction, a new constitution was adopted. Taxes were reduced, and several concessions were made to Jewish sensitivities, preserving their traditional religious rights within a framework of Roman rule. Antipater was determined to prove to the Romans that he was up to the job, and in the course of the reorganisation he appointed two of his sons to key positions. Phasael, the eldest, became Prefect of Jerusalem, while Herod, his second son, was made governor of Galilee in 46 BC.

Phasael turned out to be a man of little consequence. But Herod was special. Within a decade of his initial appointment, he had become king of Judea, and his accession in 37 BC heralded the beginning of a new era of peace and prosperity for the whole of the eastern part of the Roman empire. Like many client kings of the time, Herod was never an absolute ruler, but was simply the agent through whom Rome ruled his country. To be successful, a king needed to maintain law and order in his territory. If unable to do so, he could expect to be deposed. It was a continual balancing act, for Herod in particular. For he had to try and please both Romans and Jews, something that was virtually impossible.

Herod was one of the successful kings. Later to be known as Herod the Great, he was responsible for many striking achievements. Thoroughly at home in Hellenistic culture, he inaugurated prestigious building projects not only in his own territory, but in other cities throughout the empire. In Jerusalem, he had the water supply completely redesigned, and this and other public works provided employment for more than 50,000 men who otherwise would certainly have been unemployed. His policies were so effective that twice during his reign he actually reduced taxes: by a third in 20 BC, and

The Herodium: seat of the Herods in New Testament times, and where John the Baptist was imprisoned and beheaded.

another fourth six years later. Augustus, who was by now Roman emperor, was so impressed that he actually added to Herod's territory, and instructed the procurator of Syria to consult with him on all important matters.

For all his greatness, when Herod died in 4 BC he had few friends. He had been an outstanding statesman, soldier, and builder. But he was also an uncompromisingly ruthless man. His basic objectives were very simple: to get as much power, glory, and pleasure for himself as was humanly possible. One of his first actions on becoming king was to order the deaths of 45 members of the traditional Jewish law-making body, the Sanhedrin, allegedly for opposing his appointment. His personal life was also marred by the most extraordinary tragedy – much of it of his own making. He ruthlessly and systematically exterminated even members of his own family, including his wife Mariamne, and his two sons Alexander and Aristobulus. Only five days before his own death, he ordered the execution of Antipater, the son who would naturally have succeeded him.

Few people mourned his passing. The Jews always had a love-hate relationship with Herod. He earned their undying gratitude for the grand new temple which he began to build in Jerusalem – a structure that, it was claimed, was even more magnificent than the legendary splendour of the first temple built by Solomon. But Herod was not really a Jew. He pretended he was, and often went out of his way to try and win the admiration of his subjects. Augustus once commented that he

would rather be Herod's pig than his son – because he ostentatiously refrained from eating pork. As far as we can tell, Herod observed much, if not all, of the Jewish ritual law, and when Gentiles wanted to marry into his family he insisted they too should be circumcised and accept the Jewish faith.

But historically, his family were actually Idumeans – and in pious Jewish eyes, no amount of professed commitment to the Jewish cause could ever possibly alter that. Especially in view of the fact that to many people, he had exterminated the rightful Hasmonean rulers of Judea in order to establish his own position. In addition, many of Herod's actions did little to commend him to his Jewish subjects. He introduced new coinage which did not go quite so far as incorporating his own image (that

would have been idolatrous in Jewish eyes), but was still of a thoroughly Hellenistic design. His own court was also modelled on the Greek pattern, and seized for itself many of the political and judicial functions of the old Jewish Sanhedrin. Most of the key posts in his kingdom were awarded to non-Jews, and Herod's own sons were given a Greek education, with three of them sent to school in Rome itself. Even his army was completely non-Jewish, with Roman military instructors, and its authority was total, effectively reducing Judea to the level of a police state.

Herod's final will (his fourth) stipulated that his kingdom should be divided up among his three remaining sons, Archelaus, Antipas, and Philip. Antipas decided to dispute the will, wanting to keep it all for himself. His two brothers were

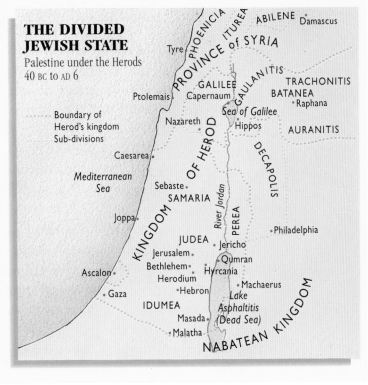

THE DIVIDED JEWISH STATE

Palestine under the Herods
40 BC to AD 6

Boundary of Herod's kingdom
Sub-divisions

forced to go to Rome to plead their own cause – and in the meantime, the country fell into chaos with Roman troops being called in to crush several revolts. In the event, Archelaus was made ruler of Judea, with the title of 'ethnarch'. Antipas became 'tetrarch' of Galilee and Perea, and Philip became 'tetrarch' of Iturea and Trachonitis (territory to the north-east of Palestine).

This was the world into which Jesus was born, and the political structures established then are reflected in the gospel stories. Archelaus did not last long: by AD 6 he had been replaced by a Roman official and Judea was declared a province of the empire. These Roman procurators introduced many reforms into the taxation system in Judea, and were responsible for considerable improvements in many areas of organisation. But they were never liked, simply because they were Romans. Philip stayed in power until AD 34, and Antipas until AD 39. It was Herod Antipas who had John the Baptist executed, and who was later involved in the trials of Jesus himself. Philip and Antipas both embarked on extensive building programmes. Antipas was responsible for the redevelopment of Sepphoris, just a few kilometres away from Nazareth, and the building of Tiberias on the western shore of the Sea of Galilee. This was a Greek city in both design and culture, and Antipas eventually made it his capital. Philip for his part rebuilt the ancient town of Panias near the source of the Jordan, and renamed it Caesarea Philippi in honour of himself and the emperor Tiberius. He also enlarged Bethsaida, and called it Julias, after Tiberius's grand-daughter.

Joseph was an ordinary working person. Artists have often depicted him as a skilled craftsman in wood, but in reality he was probably a general builder – master of many trades around the town of Nazareth. It was a good time to be a builder in Galilee. There was plenty of work in the region just at that time, and Joseph probably had a monopoly on small-scale construction work in his own small village. He and Mary are unlikely to have been extremely poor, but at the same time, Jesus was certainly not born into a situation of great material prosperity. Nor was his birth in Bethlehem in a place of his parents' choosing.

TIMES AND PLACES

The king at the time was Herod the Great. He was only half-Jewish, and deeply resented by many of his subjects. But he was the best that could be hoped for, with the real power being exercised from Rome, through a network of local officials who were responsible for the smooth operation of the empire. Augustus, who was emperor when Jesus was born, had a great fondness for gathering statistics, and according to Luke's gospel Jesus' birth was in Bethlehem rather than Nazareth because a census was being conducted, organised by an imperial representative named Quirinius. Other documents of the time show that a man of this name was indeed sent to Syria and Judea to take a census shortly after the beginning of the Christian era, perhaps around AD 6 or 7, which is of course later than the date of which Luke writes. Some have seen a problem in this, concluding that perhaps Luke got his facts wrong, or misunderstood other information as he copied it down. It is of course true that Luke was not a citizen of Palestine at the time, and must certainly have depended on other sources as he wrote his own stories. It would not have been difficult to make such a historical slip. But in general, Luke was not that kind of person, and in other parts of his writings he shows himself to have taken great care to get things right. This is particularly the case in the companion volume to Luke's gospel, the Acts of the Apostles, where he is meticulous in his descriptions of Roman officials and their titles. We also need to remember that taking a census in the ancient Roman empire was quite different from doing the same thing in a modern western democratic state. For one thing, very few people, if any at all, actually wanted to co-operate. A census could only mean one thing: the extraction of yet more taxes. As a result, people could – and did – make things difficult. In addition, without the advantage of instant communications, even a successful census could take some considerable time from start to finish. One such census in Gaul took 40 years, because of the combination of these two factors! It is quite possible that the census being taken at the time of Jesus' birth was indeed the same one as Quirinius completed several years later, using statistics collected over an extended period of time.

There are intricate historical debates surrounding the precise date of Jesus' birth, and there can legitimately be diverse opinions on such matters. But we can be quite certain of one thing: Jesus was not born at exactly the point where BC changed into AD. According to all our information, Jesus was born during the reign of Herod the Great. He died in 4 BC, and it is likely that Jesus' birth was a year or two before that. Some have claimed that this date is confirmed by the Bible stories about the wise men, astrologers who travelled from the east in pursuit of a strange star. In 7 BC there was indeed a striking conjunction of Jupiter, Saturn and Mars, something that happens only every 805 years.

But whether that had any connection with the special star of the Bible story is anyone's guess.

Whatever the resolution of these complex arguments, both Matthew and Luke (the only two gospels that contain stories of Jesus' birth) place the event in Bethlehem. This was the home city of Joseph's family, and unlike Nazareth it had a long and illustrious history. It had been the family home of king David, one of Israel's greatest heroes, and for that reason among others, some of the Old Testament prophets had looked to Bethlehem as a place where the longed-for Messiah would be born.

Today, the story of Jesus' birth is celebrated in a grand manner. But the reality was rather different. This was no glamorous Hollywood-style epic. Quite the reverse. After a long and dangerous journey, Joseph and Mary found themselves out in the street, unable to gain access even to the normal hospitality

JOHN THE BAPTIST AND JESUS

The gospels describe John the Baptist in much the same way as the Old Testament depicts the prophets. For modern readers, the word "prophet" often conjures up the picture of a spiritual star-gazer, mystically peering into a distant and uncertain future in the effort to foretell events yet to come. But the prophets of Israel were quite different. Motivated by a deep commitment to their nation, they were at least as conscious of their nation's past as of its future. They knew only too well that people can easily lose their way, and their particular calling was to summon their nation back to its moral and spiritual roots. John was the same. His message contained an uncompromising demand for integrity that went far beyond the mere performance of perfunctory religious rituals. Matthew's gospel reports some strong language on his

lips, especially about the religious leaders, Pharisees and Sadducees, who John felt were more concerned about external rites than true moral goodness. More than half a millenium earlier, the prophet Micah had said pretty much the same thing, as he asked "Will the Lord be pleased if I bring him thousands of sheep or endless streams of olive-oil?" – and then went on to declare, "No, the Lord has told us what is good. What he requires of us is this: to do what is just, to show constant love, and to live in humble fellowship with our God" (Micah 6:7-8). Micah had also looked forward to a time when God would appoint a ruler to bring peace and justice to the nations. John saw himself as the messenger running before God's appointee, preparing the way for Jesus. He carried his message throughout the land: not only in the valley of the river Jordan, but also

into Samaritan territory (John 3:23). Eventually, he fell foul of the authorities. Herod Antipas saw him as a threat – both politically and morally – and had him arrested, imprisoned in the fortress of Machaerus by the Dead Sea, and ultimately executed there.

Antipas needed to curb John's activities partly because he was successful at gathering large numbers of followers. The Jewish historian Josephus described him as "a good man who bade the Jews practise virtue, be just to one another, and pious towards God, and come together by means of baptism" (*Antiquities* 18.117). This seems to imply that he actually founded some kind of religious community, entered presumably through baptism. This fact has led some to connect him with the community of Essenes who lived by the Dead Sea at Qumran, who compiled the Dead Sea Scrolls, and used water quite extensively in their complex religious rituals. But automatically offered to travellers in the middle east. Crowded out of the inns and hotels, they were forced to spend the night in a stable – and that was where Jesus was born. The gospels do not actually mention a stable, but if the new-born child was placed in a manger then presumably he was among facilities intended for animals. As early as the second century AD, tradition suggested the stable was actually a cave. Perhaps a place where a poor family shared living space with their own animals – and were persuaded to admit the desperate couple whose child was about to be born. Certainly, Jesus was born among ordinary people in fairly run-down conditions. As he himself later said, "Foxes have holes, and birds have nests, but the Son of Man has nowhere to lie down and rest" (Matthew 8:20).

The young parents and their baby may have seemed like vagrants. But to those with the eyes to see, this was an event of the

apart from the fact that both they and John used water for religious purposes, they have little in common. Their baptismal practices were quite different, John stressing a call to a once-for-all radical repentance and change of life, whereas the Essene washings were repeated many times, perhaps daily. Nor did the Essene community need a figure like John: for them, baptism was a self-administered rite. And, unlike the Essenes, John was not calling people to withdraw from ordinary life to await the coming of God's Messiah. On the contrary, he announced the coming of God's Kingdom, which would both transform and undermine the prevailing order of things. There is, however, evidence of a continuing movement associated with John the Baptist. When the Christian evangelist St Paul arrived in Ephesus in Asia Minor some 50 years later, he discovered a group of religious believers who identified themselves

as followers of John – though when they heard Paul's message about Jesus as Messiah, they became Christians.

Like many people of great faith, John also had his moments of questioning doubt. Matthew and Luke record how he sent some of his own disciples to ask Jesus, "Are you the one John said was going to come, or should we expect someone else?" (Luke 7:18). No doubt John was in prison at the time, and was wondering whether his life's work had been in vain – for it seemed that God's Kingdom had not arrived after all. Perhaps John was expecting a military ruler, like so many others of his day. But Jesus' answer was meant to reassure him: "Go back and tell John what you have seen and heard: the blind can see, the lame can walk, those who suffer from dreaded skin diseases are made clean, the deaf can hear, the dead are raised to life, and the Good News is preached to the poor." All of them signs that God had

indeed intervened with power in the life of his people.

The story of John's death is recorded in three of the gospels (Matthew, Mark, and Luke), and tells how Herod Antipas's daughter, dancing at a party, demanded John's head on a plate from her drunken father. She got her wish: an unworthy end for a man who stood in a unique position between two ages of human history. For later generations have looked back to him as the one who first recognised Jesus as the Messiah and Saviour of the world.

most breathtaking significance. The shepherds discovered the meaning of it all by the same means as Mary and Joseph, as angels brought them the good news. Far away, unidentified wise men recognised that something important was taking place – and headed for Palestine. Making straight for Jerusalem, the king's capital, they looked for this special child. The Bible does not actually say there were three of them, nor does it identify them as kings. But since they brought three gifts, it was natural to assume they were three in number (though some traditions have twelve). And there were any number of Old Testament texts that were soon understood to be referring to kings from all over the earth coming to pay homage to Jesus the Messiah.

As so often happens, the New Testament writers say little or nothing to satisfy the curiosity of modern readers, who always want to know more. In Matthew's gospel, the focus of attention soon

The River Jordan near Tel Dan in the north of Israel.

shifts to another king, far closer at hand, and much more dangerous. On hearing of the alleged prophecies, Herod the Great was himself curious – for all the wrong reasons. The idea that his own position might be threatened – even by a new-born baby – was something he could not tolerate, and Matthew records the

HOME & FAMILY LIFE IN NAZARETH

The New Testament tells us virtually nothing at all about Jesus' life as a child. The typical house of the time would be flat-roofed, with one room in which the family ate, slept, and carried on their business. Various statements in the gospels imply that Jesus followed in the footsteps of Joseph, carrying on trade as a *tekton*. This Greek word has often been translated "carpenter" – and it would certainly include working with wood. But it would involve more than that, and Jesus was probably a general builder. At the time when he was growing up, the ancient city of Sepphoris was being redesigned and rebuilt just 7 or 8 kilometres from Nazareth – a project which must have created enormous employment opportunities for all kinds of skilled craftspeople. The city was finished just shortly before Jesus began his public ministry of teaching, and it is interesting to speculate that both he and some of his band of disciples may well have been thrown out of work at that time as the massive project was completed. It could also be that Joseph died about this time. He certainly seems to have been dead by the time Jesus began his public ministry of teaching and healing, for he never features in the later stories of Jesus' adult life. Whenever Jesus' family are mentioned, it is only ever

Mary and his brothers and sisters (Matthew 12:46, Mark 3:31, Luke 8:19). At his death, Jesus as the elder son of the family asked one of his disciples to take care of his mother Mary – another indication that Joseph was by that time dead.

Jesus obviously grew up in a simple home environment. But he also had the opportunity to gain some education. He was competent enough to read the ancient scriptures in Hebrew at the local synagogue. There were organised schools in Palestine at this period, but most boys would receive their education in the synagogue. In any case, Galilee was the kind of place where everyday life provided its own liberal education. Quite remote from the centres of power in Judea and Jerusalem, Galilee had a considerable non-Jewish population. It was on some of the major trading routes between east and west, and Jesus must have come into contact with people of many different races there. Greek, the international language of the empire, would frequently be heard on the streets of Galilee, and it is quite likely that Jesus knew Greek – as well as Hebrew and Aramaic. Aramaic was the language most Jewish people spoke at home. This had originally been popularised by the Persian empire in

the fifth and sixth centuries BC as its own international language. It was quite similar to Hebrew in many ways, and in the centuries before the birth of Jesus had been widely adopted throughout Palestine.

Jesus was not the only child in his family. Mark 6:3 tells us that when, as an adult teacher, he returned to Nazareth, people found it hard to accept his message, because "Isn't he the carpenter, the son of Mary, and the brother of James, Joseph, Judas, and Simon ? Aren't his sisters living here?" We know little else about these brothers and sisters, though they were apparently believers in the very earliest days of the church (Acts 1:14). James ultimately headed up the church in Jerusalem. But even he was not a disciple during Jesus' lifetime, and only came to accept Jesus as Messiah as a result of a special encounter with the risen Jesus after the crucifixion and resurrection (1 Corinthians 15:7). Mary herself must have been torn between discipleship and doubt, as she struggled to balance the needs of various members of her family circle. But she was very firmly on Jesus' side, and features in the book of Acts as one of the leaders of the infant church in Jerusalem (Acts 1:14).

Religiously, Jesus' family were obviously committed Jewish believers. Some of them may have been Pharisees. James was certainly a conservative character, even later as grisly story of how he ordered the massacre of all the baby boys two years old or younger (Matthew 2:16-18). There is no mention of any such thing in other sources of the day. But historians are agreed that Herod could easily have come up with such an evil plan. He had an insane fear of any threat to his life and power –

a Christian, and according to one of his later biographers he spent so much time praying in the temple that his knees were like camel's knees! He was able to stay on in Jerusalem after many other Christian leaders – including middle-of-the-road Jewish believers like Peter –

were forced to quit. All of this implies he must have been quite traditional. Certainly if some of Jesus' closest relatives were Pharisees, that could explain why he so often singled them

Jewish children at play in the street in Jerusalem.

out for special condemnation: they were the one Jewish group about whom he knew the most, because of his own first-hand experience.

The fact that the New Testament contains so little about Jesus' life as a youth prompted later generations to produce their own imaginary accounts of what he was like. From the second century and later, several such stories survive, with exotic titles like *The Gospel of the Nativity of Mary, The History of Joseph the Carpenter*, and *The Childhood Gospel of Thomas* (not to be confused with *The Gospel of Thomas*, which is a different kind of document altogether). These 'gospels' contain legendary stories, mostly concerned with proving that Jesus had miraculous powers even as a child – powers, they claim, that he used even then to bring embarrassment both to his family and to the religious establishment. But such accounts are no more than fabrication, written by committed believers in the effort both to satisfy curiosity and to enhance Jesus' reputation.

real or imaginary — and it is not difficult to believe that a king who made a habit of murdering his own children could readily do the same to other people's.

Jesus and his parents escaped from this threat, as Joseph received yet another angelic message warning them to leave the country and head for Egypt (Matthew 2:13-15). The precise details of the journey are obscure. It would certainly have been quite a long trip, though a shorter distance than that from Nazareth to Bethlehem. But Matthew's main purpose in reporting it is to show how some key events in Jesus' life ran parallel to the experiences of the nation of Israel in the Old Testament. Of course, Matthew — like the other gospel writers — was telling his story with the benefit of hindsight. In the light of the whole course of Jesus' life, death and resurrection it seemed obvious that God was present with him in a special way. The first disciples had little difficulty in believing that he was actually the Messiah and Son of God. And as they reviewed his own story, it was obvious to them that God had been there right from the beginning. Through the various angels, announcing his conception, reassuring Mary and Joseph, ensuring his continued safety, and sharing the good news not only with pious souls in the Jewish community, but even — through the wise men — with the world at large.

PRIORITIES FOR LIFE

After the stories of how Jesus was born, and later taken to the temple to be blessed, the gospels generally jump over something like 30 years, and by the time they pick up the story in any detail he was a fully grown adult. Luke summarises Jesus' childhood in a single sentence: "The child grew and became strong; he was full of wisdom, and God's blessings were upon him" (Luke 2:40). There is just one story, relating to the time when Jesus was twelve years old and went up to Jerusalem with his family, to celebrate the feast of Passover (Luke 2:41-52). At this age, he would be ready to take his place as a man in the Jewish religious community. He clearly had a good understanding of the ancestral faith of his people, and when he engaged in discussion with the theological experts in the temple they were surprised by his perceptions. But he had never been formally taught by any of the leading rabbis, and his religious education would mostly be gained in the home, from his mother.

The fact that Jesus had no formal religious training amazed all those who heard him as an adult. But before he could begin his life's work in religious teaching, Jesus needed to clarify his own priorities. The first challenge came when his own cousin, John the Baptist, began delivering remarkable messages declaring that his own nation was about to meet with the judgment of God. This was nothing specially surprising, for the prophets of the Old Testament had frequently made similar announcements, linking social and political tragedy with moral and spiritual disobedience. John certainly identified himself with these characters. He copied both his dress (camel's hair cloth) and his diet (locusts and wild honey) from Elijah, the most uncompromising prophet of all and, like him, delivered his message in the desert.

John's demand was simple: "Turn away from your sins and be baptised, and God will forgive your sins" (Luke 3:3). Many did just that, though others were hesitant about it. After *Bethlehem* all, baptism was a ceremony most closely associated *at sunrise.* with the admission of non-Jewish people to the Jewish

"WHEN GOD BECAME A CHILD"

Modern readers of the gospels often wish that they told us more details about Jesus' childhood. But in the ancient world, childhood was never given much value. In many parts of the Roman empire, children were regularly exploited and marginalised. In sophisticated Greek and Roman communities, unwanted children were often abandoned shortly after birth. Sometimes to die, often to be snatched by gangs of beggars who would mutilate them or raise them as prostitutes. Even in a caring environment, being a child was always regarded as merely a preparation for being an adult – and only adults (especially men) could be truly important.

In the light of these facts, what surprises us is not how little, but how much the gospels say about Jesus' birth and childhood. Long before his conception, angels appear to Mary and others, to announce that this child would be special in every way. We may be curious about Jesus' childhood, but we still tend to think of Jesus accomplishing great things as an adult – and his childhood, therefore, was but the essential means to that end. But for Luke in particular, Jesus the baby was as important as Jesus the adult. Throughout their stories of his birth, the New Testament writers emphasise that God was fully and truly with the baby in Bethlehem. When Jesus was brought to the temple for blessing after his birth, the old man Simeon praised God that the new age of God's Kingdom had arrived: "With my own eyes I have seen your salvation ... " (Luke 2:30). He did not pray for a few more years, so he could see the adult Jesus fulfil the aspirations of his people: he affirmed that the promise had already come true.

Coming to terms with such claims was not easy. Even in the earliest Christian communities, there were plenty of people who could readily accept that God was fully and absolutely present in the life of the adult Jesus, but who found it impossible that the same could be true either of the infant at Bethlehem or of the young child Jesus. Even some of the church's leaders in the early centuries could not come to terms with such a staggering affirmation. It was hard enough to believe that God could become human at all. But for a child to be fully and truly divine? That was pushing things just too far. And so there developed a powerful theological lobby who tried to argue that actually God had only entered into the human Jesus when he became an adult. Perhaps it happened at his baptism, or at some other point – there were various theories – but in no way could the child Jesus have been fully divine from the outset.

Arguments of this sort surfaced quite early in the church's life. Certainly by the end of the first century. In the New Testament, 1 John was written partly to tackle such ideas, put forward by those who came to be known as Docetists, because they argued Jesus only "seemed" (the Greek word is *dokeo*) to be divine, but wasn't really. By the time Luke was writing his gospel, some were already questioning whether the baby of Bethlehem could really have been divine. Perhaps that is why this gospel lays so much emphasis on the stories of Jesus' birth.

Two thousand years later, most Christians have yet to realise the full implications of all this. But if "the medium is the message", then the key to understanding much of the story of Jesus is to be found here. God chose the most ordinary of ways in which to break into our world. An ordinary family. An ordinary baby. These two things become central to the whole of the rest of the story. For the gospels show how it was ordinary people, of many different sorts and backgrounds, who responded most eagerly to Jesus' message. More than once, Jesus singled out a child as a model of the true disciple, and his total picture of God was rooted in that weakness and vulnerability that can be seen most clearly in the person of a child.

Later theological statements – and many popular Christmas carols – claim that in Jesus, "God became a man". At best, that is a half-truth. It is certainly not the message of the gospels. Notwithstanding all the questions such a statement might raise in our minds, they unhesitatingly declare that "God became a child". Grasping that will begin to bring us close to the heart of the true meaning of Jesus' life and teaching.

faith – hardly something that those who were born Jews would
readily submit themselves to. But Jesus had no such hesitation,
and insisted on identifying himself with those sincere souls who
were looking for a new start in life – and so he came to John for
baptism.

All four gospels depict Jesus' baptism as the point
at which his life's work was first identified. Two
quotations from the Old Testament came together in

*The Judean Desert, with
Wadi Makuk seen from
the air.*

the heavenly voice which announced, "You are my own dear Son. I am pleased with you." The one, from Psalm 2 :7, was regarded as a prophecy of the coming Messiah. The other, from Isaiah 42:1, referred to God's servant, who would suffer on behalf of other people. Both of them together emphasizing that while he would be the Messiah, Jesus would not easily fit the expected stereotypes of a conquering king. Instead, he would be a different kind of Messiah, and he would do God's will through suffering and service.

Immediately following his baptism, Jesus had to sort out his personal priorities in the temptations. Mark mentions these only briefly, but Matthew and Luke both give detailed accounts. All three place this period of self-appraisal at the very start of Jesus' public work, as a programmatic statement of his basic aims and objectives. But the issues raised in this story were continually cropping up throughout his ministry.

The first temptation was to make stones into bread. Several Old Testament texts seemed to imply that when the Messiah came, he would feed hungry people (Isaiah 25:6-8, 49:9-10, Ezekiel 39:17-20). Since Jesus was in the desert at the time, he was no doubt personally hungry anyway. And he was certainly not indifferent to the physical needs of starving people. Later stories show him feeding the hungry in various contexts. But to establish a reputation on this basis alone would have been to deny the very essence of what God was calling him to do. He dismissed the temptation with other words from the Old Testament: "... one does not live by bread alone, but by every word that comes from the mouth of the Lord" (Deuteronomy 8:3).

A similar temptation presented itself with the suggestion that he should throw himself down from one of the towers of the temple in Jerusalem. If he survived, that would certainly have been a dramatic demonstration to the whole nation that he was indeed endued with special powers. Into the bargain, there was at least one Old Testament prophecy which seemed to suggest the Messiah would appear in such a dramatic way in the temple (Malachi 3:1). This, together with another promise that God would protect those who trusted him (Psalm 91), presented a powerful argument for putting God to the test. If Jesus really was the Messiah, should he not confirm this calling by trying out these promises to see if God was truly on his side? Jesus was not afraid of the miraculous and the supernatural: there are many examples of exactly that in the rest of his life. But he rejected the temptation to base his message purely on such sensationalism – again quoting an Old Testament text to back up his judgment: "Do not put the Lord your God to the test ... " (Deuteronomy 6:16).

Finally, the temptation to be the kind of Messiah figure most Jews were looking for: a political deliverer. If he would worship the devil, then he could have all the kingdoms of the world. Including Rome. Attractive though it was, Jesus rejected this proposition. First, because he could not share sovereignty with the devil. And secondly, because he knew that the structure of God's kingdom was to be quite different from the kind of authority to be found in an empire like the Romans had. It was not too difficult to reject this temptation. But it was the one that kept coming back time and time again in a particularly powerful fashion. And Jesus dismissed it most categorically, again quoting

HOW DO WE KNOW ABOUT JESUS?

One of the surprising things about the New Testament is that it contains four different accounts of the life and teaching of Jesus. The gospels – Matthew, Mark, Luke and John – all tell the story of Jesus in their own different ways. They are like four different portraits, each depicting him from the angle that seemed most interesting to their various writers.

We will ask how trustworthy these portraits are in a later chapter. But there can be no doubt they are deeply personal representations of their subject. Each of the four writers was a Christian disciple, writing his own story for a variety of purposes. Luke seems to have intended to explain the person and teaching of Jesus for

intelligent Roman and Greek readers such as Theophilus, the person to whom his book is addressed (Luke 1:1). John, for his part, hoped to convince his readers that "Jesus is the Messiah, the Son of God, and that through your faith in him you may have life" (John 20:31). Neither Matthew nor Mark actually states his purpose, but it is widely believed that Matthew wrote for Jewish Christians who wanted to know how Jesus the Messiah related to their traditional beliefs – while Mark's considerable emphasis on discipleship seems to suggest that he was writing for Christians, to encourage them in their faith, perhaps at a time when some of them were suffering persecution.

The different emphases of each of the gospels implies that they were composed to meet the needs of people living in different cultures around the Roman empire. Matthew, with its strong Jewish emphasis and many quotations from the Old Testament, certainly relates to the life of the Jewish Christian churches, and it is not difficult to imagine that it must have been written in Palestine itself.

Its careful structure, and the way Jesus' teaching is presented in a topical format, has led many to conclude that it was originally produced as a teaching manual for the instruction of new converts in the church.

Mark, on the other hand, frequently explains Jewish traditions and customs for the benefit of readers who were clearly unfamiliar with such things. All of which

A Galilee fisherman hauls in his catch in the early morning light.

strongly suggests that Mark was writing for a non-Jewish audience. Other New Testament mentions of a person called Mark link him with Rome, and it is widely believed that this is where Mark's gospel was written. Mark has a very accessible picture of Jesus. Rough and ready, one could almost say. Some of the early church historians explained this by the fact that they believed it to be the reminiscences of Peter, taken down and edited by his friend John Mark.

Luke was obviously at home in a sophisticated Roman context. Not perhaps in Rome itself. But there can be no doubt that Luke was very much a part of Hellenistic society. He himself is probably the only non-Jewish author in the New Testament, and from a literary standpoint, Luke's Greek style is among the most refined in the entire Bible. He obviously had a great breadth of vision, and was particularly concerned with the ways Jesus' ministry and message related to the marginalised and disadvantaged peoples of the world – as well as with the spiritual roots of Jesus' lifestyle. Prayer and experience of the Holy Spirit play a leading role in Luke's portrait of Jesus.

Then there is John. Undoubtedly different from the other three in both style and content. Its tone is far more reflective than the others, and the place of action also differs, with much more about Jesus' activities in Jerusalem, and correspondingly less about Galilee. Fifty years ago, historians doubted the accuracy of John on this basis. But today the tables have been turned, and John is highly regarded as an independent, but no less valuable, witness to the life and teaching of Jesus. Probably written in two separate editions, John originated in Palestine in a Jewish context, but was later revised and updated (by its original author) to be utilised in a Hellenistic city elsewhere an Old Testament scripture: "Worship the Lord your God and serve only him."

Matthew and Luke depict Jesus in a kind of personal combat with the devil himself. But more often, these questions, and others like them, were raised by ordinary people with whom Jesus came into contact day by day. Even his own special friends at times misunderstood what he was saying, both about himself and about God's Kingdom.

DISCIPLES

It was not at all difficult for a religious teacher in first century Palestine to get others to follow him. There was such a ferment of spiritual expectancy at the time that many people were constantly on the lookout for anyone who could give them new direction and fresh hope. John the Baptist had already attracted his own band of followers long before Jesus appeared on the scene. According to the gospel of John, some of them formed the core for Jesus' own group of personal friends, the twelve disciples.

in the empire. Tradition connects John with Ephesus in Asia Minor.

There is obviously a complex interrelationship between the various gospels. Luke and John both say that they used sources for their work, much like any modern historian would (Luke 1:1-4, John 21:25). The three gospels of Matthew, Mark and Luke are so similar that they have been called the 'synoptic gospels'. Their writers must have shared some of the same source materials. Just about the whole of Mark is contained (often word-for-word) in Matthew and Luke, while Matthew and Luke themselves have much common material (again, frequently word-for-word) that is not found in Mark. One popular way of explaining this is to suppose that Mark was written first, then Matthew and Luke both utilised Mark's story in writing their own. But

they supplemented Mark's story with the other materials they both have in common (mostly teaching) – a source often labelled 'Q', for no other reason than that the German word for 'source' begins with that letter! At one time, it was thought that Matthew and Luke sat with piles of

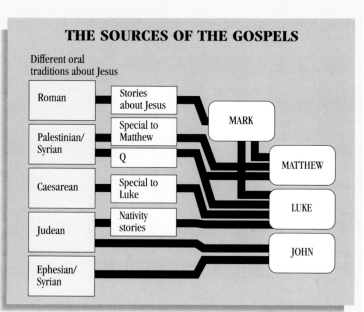

THE SOURCES OF THE GOSPELS

36

Jesus' message is neatly summarised by Mark: "The right time has come, and the Kingdom of God is near! Turn away from your sins and believe the Good News" (Mark 1:14). That message could be understood by different people in different ways. Some were no doubt attracted by the thought that the Kingdom of God would overthrow the kingdom of Rome, and establish in its place an autonomous Jewish state once more. Others were drawn in by the more spiritual demand that people should be prepared to change their lifestyle and orient it in new directions. Yet others

Trajan's column silhouetted against the sunset at Ephesus, Turkey.

documents before them, snipping out bits and pieces here and there and glueing them all together. But it would be more complex than that. They may well not have had source documents at all, but were simply drawing on stories and teachings they had heard repeated in the same familiar words in many Christian gatherings.

How we think the gospels were written obviously determines when we think they were written. A majority view today places Mark first, around AD 65, followed by Matthew sometime in the mid-70s AD, then Luke perhaps ten years later. John is more difficult to date. If he knew of the three synoptic gospels, and even perhaps used them, then obviously we would need to date his work towards the end of the first century – a view that also correlates with the

traditions of the early church, which pictured John as an aged apostle writing his gospel at the end of his life. But there is other evidence to suggest a much earlier date for John. Some reputable scholars have even claimed it was the very first gospel to be written, sometime in the mid-40s AD. It is not as easy to date the gospels as it once was. Perhaps the most we can say is that they were all written sometime between about AD

40 and AD 80 – and a growing number of experts would place all four of them very firmly in the earlier years of that period.

simply found themselves fascinated by Jesus, and wanted to be with him. It was this that led Simon and his brother Andrew to become disciples. Walking by the shore of lake Galilee, Jesus identified them as skilful men, with many talents that could be used in his work. "You're good at catching fish", he told them: "Come with me, and I will teach you to catch people". Without any further ado, they agreed to follow him. The same thing happened with two other brothers, James and John. And no doubt many other more anonymous characters as well.

There was a lot Jesus wanted these people to learn. Facts, about himself and their place in God's Kingdom. New perceptions of themselves, and of the world and its people. And new forms of obedience to God's will. But Jesus asked for none of these things at this stage. Their enthusiasm was the thing that counted most of all. There was no demand that they undergo some fancy religious ritual. No requirement that they sever all ties with their previous friends. No insistence that they do any more than they were happy to do at that stage of their understanding of Jesus. As the story progresses, we can see how they made many mistakes. They were occasionally ashamed of their behaviour and their lack of spiritual sensitivity. But they responded to what Jesus was offering them. A new experience of the power of God working in their nation, and the opportunity to give their strength and their talents to a cause that was not only worthwhile, but personally fulfilling: the Kingdom of God itself.

ACCEPTANCE
IN GALILEE

THE TRAVELS OF JESUS

ONSIDERING THE enormous influence Jesus has exerted over the whole course of world civilisation, it is hard to believe that during his lifetime he scarcely moved away from his home province of Galilee. Galilee itself was a small place – not more than about 70 by 40 kilometres. And even within this constricted area, the majority of Jesus' activities took place around the northern end of the Sea of Galilee – mostly near to the town of Capernaum, which seems to have been his home base. According to the gospels, he once travelled to Caesarea Philippi – on the eastern side of the river Jordan and about 25 kilometres from Capernaum. He also went a similar distance to the area around Tyre and Sidon, to the north-west of Galilee. Occasionally, he went to the Greek territory known as Decapolis, east of the Jordan, and *en route* paid the occasional visit to the fishing town of Bethsaida.

When Jesus went to Jerusalem, he may have

Spring flowers on the shore of the Sea of Galilee.

taken the longer route through the eastern district of Perea, though he is more likely to have gone directly south, through Samaria. We do not know for certain how many trips Jesus made to Jerusalem. The three synoptic gospels of Matthew, Mark and Luke show him going there only once, on the occasion when he was arrested and eventually crucified. But the fourth gospel, John, has Jesus in Jerusalem on several occasions, while Matthew and Luke both have him refer to his wish to nurture Jerusalem and its people "many times" (Matthew 23:27, Luke 13:34). So we may assume that he had been to the city before his trial and death. But going on pilgrimage there was certainly not a major priority in his life.

Jews of the southern province of Judea would always make a special effort to worship in the temple at Jerusalem at least once a year. But the inhabitants of Galilee were much less likely to do so. Galilean people had more relaxed attitudes to many things, and religious tradition was one of them. When Jesus later questioned the accepted positions on all sorts of issues, ranging from the

GALILEE

For most people, Galilee probably conjures up images of peaceful seaside scenes, with fishermen quietly going about their work in as idyllic a situation as you could imagine. It is certainly true that the Sea of Galilee dominates much of the landscape in this part of Palestine. The Sea itself is not particularly extensive, only a matter of some 18 kilometres long and no more than about 11 kilometres across at its widest point, while the deepest part is about 62 metres. It has had several names. The original Hebrew designation was Sea of Chinnereth, derived from the word Kinnor, meaning a lyre or harp (its shape vaguely resembles such an instrument). The New Testament also calls it Gennesaret and the Sea of Tiberias, while it is also . occasionally designated a "lake" rather than a "sea".

It was an ideal place for the kind of itinerant teaching ministry that Jesus had, and the gospels often depict him teaching from a boat to crowds gathered on the shore. Modern pilgrims can see several places on the western side of the Sea where the mountains form a kind of natural theatre, and the voice of someone speaking on a boat can be clearly heard on the shore.

The whole area was also a pleasant place to live and work, with a sub-tropical climate easily sustaining regular crops of dates and bananas. The Jewish historian Josephus enthused about its many natural attractions: "... the whole area is excellent for crops or pasturage and rich in trees of every kind, so that by its fertility it invites even those least inclined to work on the land. In fact, every inch of it has been cultivated by the inhabitants, and not a parcel goes to waste. It is thickly covered with towns, and thanks to the natural abundance of the soil, the many villages are so densely populated that the smallest of them has more than fifteen thousand inhabitants." (*Jewish War* 3.42-3)

Even if Josephus was exaggerating a little, it was obviously an idyllic place to live. Galilee fell naturally into two parts. Upper Galilee was a mountainous area, rising from 1000 metres above sea level to over 3000, and in the time of Jesus would be predominantly forest. Few people sabbath day to food laws, this was just what many Galileans wanted to hear.

ALL IN A DAY'S WORK

What was a typical day like in the life of Jesus? Right at the beginning of his gospel, Mark gives an account of such a day (Mark 1:21-39). There were just two major aspects of his activities: teaching and healing, words and deeds. Both went hand in hand, and both were essential elements in Jesus' entire ministry.

The particular day described by Mark was a sabbath, and began in the synagogue at Capernaum. The sabbath was a holy day, whose origins were traced by the Jews right back to creation itself. According to the Old Testament stories, God rested on the seventh day after all the creating was done – a pattern of life that was to be adopted by everyone, and was enshrined throughout Jewish law, including the Ten Commandments. Keeping the sabbath day free of work was an important aspect of religious devotion, though in the time of Jesus the rabbis had spent much

lived there – though some did, and even today there are ruins of ancient synagogues still standing. But it was Lower Galilee that Josephus was really describing. Here, the countryside is incredibly varied, at an average of 120 metres above sea level, dipping down to 200 metres below sea level at the Sea of Galilee, while the peak of Mt Tabor rises to almost 600 metres in the south-eastern corner.

In Jesus' day Galilee had a mainly agricultural economy, and the landscape itself had a profound influence on the lifestyle of the people. There were also some hot springs just south of the city of Tiberias. Nowadays they provide a natural resource for fashionable vacation resorts, and in Roman times it was just the same. Cultured Gentiles flocked from all parts to

enjoy a luxury break at these bath-houses and villas. There is much fertile soil here too, especially around the plain of Gennesaret, which is still one of the most productive regions of modern Israel. Galilee was a small place, only about 70 by 40 kilometres. But farming was not easy everywhere. There was a lot of stony and unproductive soil, and the rainfall had wide variations, ranging from about 30 to 55 centimetres per year.

The settlements were as varied as the landscape. No two towns were exactly the same – and the people of each place had their own characteristic ways of life. The Herod family invested heavily in the construction of magnificent public buildings, following Greek and Roman styles. Tiberias could boast mosaic floors comparable with any

provincial capital in the Roman empire. But even in more homely villages in the Galilean countryside, Hellenistic influence was ever present, in both art forms and language. Galilean coins of this period had inscriptions solely in Greek, and this would be the main language of the area, though some Jews also spoke Aramaic – evidently with a strong accent (Matthew 26:73).

Galilee had always been less than purely Jewish. Hebrew tradition assigned this region to the tribes of Zebulun and Naphtali, but 700 years before the time of Christ the prophet Isaiah could write of "Galilee, where the foreigners live" (Isaiah 9:1). Down through the centuries, the Jews had a hard time in Galilee, and it was only settled systematically after the Hasmonean king Alexander Jannaeus (103-76 BC) conquered the

Top: Aerial view of the River Jordan just to the North of the Sea of Galilee.
Left: Sacks of beans and nuts in a Nazareth market
Above: The River Jordan to the south of the Sea of Galilee.

time arguing about what sort of activities could be classed as "work". There were varying opinions on this. But one thing was beyond reasonable doubt: the sabbath was, first and foremost, a day for worship. So the synagogue was an obvious place for Jesus to go on the sabbath day. Going to worship would be a sign of commitment to the religious traditions of his people. And, since everybody else would be there too, he could expect to find a ready-made audience in the local synagogue.

Modern visitors to Capernaum can still see the remains of an ancient synagogue. The present ruins date from the fourth or fifth

territory and tried to make it Jewish. Imposed settlement programmes rarely succeed, and his was no exception. In New Testament times, non-Jewish people still formed a majority of the population in many places. They lived in accordance with Hellenistic customs, they spoke Greek, and they worshipped their own traditional gods and goddesses. This was especially the case in cities like Sepphoris and Tiberias, but even in towns with a more Jewish orientation things were not much different. Galilee was a truly multicultural society, where Gentiles could live like Gentiles, Jews could live like Jews – and they could all do it more or less

Ruins of the synagogue at Chorazin in Galilee.

harmoniously. Synagogues were just as easy to find in predominantly Gentile towns like Tiberias as they were in more traditional Jewish settlements such as Capernaum. The romantic idea that Jesus lived in a rural backwater has little relation to

the facts. Galilee was the one place in Palestine where foreign influences could most readily be experienced at first hand, and we may be sure that from childhood Jesus was well acquainted with the cultural and religious values of the wider world of century AD, though the synagogue of Jesus' time may well have been on the same site. It had been built by a Roman army commander for the local people (Luke 7:1-10). This kind of collaboration between Jews and Romans would have been unthinkable for many of the pious Jews of Judea, but was typical of the more tolerant relationships between different groups in Galilean society.

Historically, Jewish worship had always centred on the temple in Jerusalem. King Solomon – legendary for his wealth – had built the first one, but Herod the Great drew up plans for a temple that would be even more splendid, though this restoration was not finished until long after his time, and only survived intact for a mere six years before it was destroyed in the fall of Jerusalem in AD 70. Herod wanted it to be a magnificent place, fit to take its place among the wonders of the Roman world, and a sanctuary where worship could authentically reflect the mystical glamour of all the ancient rituals. Every true Jewish believer – even those scattered around the Mediterranean in cities far removed from

the Roman empire.

Most Galileans were happy with this easy-going tolerance. But the more conservative Jewish authorities in Judea viewed things differently. Not that there was much they could do, for Galilee was geographically cut off from Judea by Samaria. Its relative isolation from Jerusalem was to serve the rabbis well at a later date, when they were looking for a safe haven from the turmoil of the Jewish War against the Romans in AD 66-70. But at the time of Jesus, orthodox believers did not care much for this permissive and open society. Certainly there was no expectation that the Messiah would come from Galilee, and when the sophisticated Nathanael sarcastically asked "Can anything good come from Nazareth?", he was voicing a sentiment widely held in Jerusalem

(John 1:46). To the upright city dwellers of Judea, the Galileans were very much second-class citizens. They might be stigmatised as faithless in religious observance ("people of the land"), but ironically they also had a strongly nationalistic bent, and several anti-Roman revolts had their roots in Galilee. The great revolt of AD 66 broke out here, with the historian Josephus as one of its ringleaders.

In strategic terms, Galilee was an important place. The main trade routes from north to south passed through, and it was here that Herod the Great fought his decisive battle for control of the land against the Parthians in 39-38 BC. When he died, his son Herod Antipas became "tetrarch" ("ruler of one fourth") of Galilee and Peraea (Transjordan), to be succeeded by Herod Agrippa I,

until finally in AD 44 it became a Roman province, with its own governor.

Jerusalem – aimed to visit the temple at least once in a lifetime, more often if it was practical. But for normal everyday devotion, that was impossible – and so a large network of synagogues had sprung up wherever Jewish people lived. At first, they were probably concentrated in Jewish settlements outside Palestine. But by the Christian era, even the Palestinian Jews had recognised the value of having a local place of worship. Only ten adult males were required to have a synagogue, and so every small settlement could easily have its own.

Synagogue worship was quite different from the pomp and ceremony of the temple. Instead of animal sacrifices, prayer and the reading of the scriptures were the primary activities. The sabbath was the main regular occasion for worship, and the services would be presided over by the ruler or chief officer. Jairus, whose daughter was healed by Jesus, was one such person (Mark 5:22). But the synagogue was not dominated by clergy and full-time theological experts. It was essentially a lay institution, where any male who was suitably qualified could take part in a service.

A major qualification was the ability to read the ancient scriptures in Hebrew. By the time of Jesus, this was no longer the everyday language of the people, but many boys were educated at the schools that were attached to the synagogues, and would learn to read and understand Hebrew. The synagogue always had a special welcome for a visiting teacher, and when such a person was present, the reading of the Hebrew scriptures (especially the prophetic books) would be followed by an exposition. Mark says nothing about Jesus' message in the synagogue at Capernaum, but the response of the people implies it was quite different from what they normally heard there: "the people who heard him were amazed at the way he taught, for he wasn't like the teachers of the Law; instead, he taught with authority" (Mark 1:22).

Jesus' authority was not confined to the things he said. If anything, his deeds were calculated to be even more threatening to the religious establishment. What happened next in the synagogue at Capernaum raises all sorts of questions in the minds of modern western people. But Mark records it in a matter-of-fact way. A man with an evil spirit burst into the synagogue, and announced that Jesus was "God's holy messenger" come to destroy such spirits – whereupon Jesus ordered the spirit to leave the man. Authority in teaching was one thing. But authority to cast out evil spirits was something else – and the people recognised it. Of course, Jesus was not the only wandering healer at work in Galilee. On a subsequent occasion, his disciples were concerned when they found someone else doing similar things (albeit invoking Jesus' name, Mark 9:38-40). But this was certainly not a normal part of weekly synagogue worship, and the people were amazed to see such things happening before their eyes. On subsequent occasions, Jesus' ability to heal, and his habit of doing it on the sabbath (did it qualify as "work"?), were both criticised. But at the outset of his ministry, it simply took people by surprise, and the news of what was going on soon spread.

Mark's account of the rest of this typical day continues with more healings and exorcisms. Simon Peter's mother-in-law was one of those restored to health, but she was just one of many. So many,

Fishermen preparing their nets. The River Jordan near the exit to the Sea of Galilee.

in fact, that Jesus continued working well into the evening. Not surprisingly, when the disciples found him next morning out in the countryside praying, their message was that "Everyone is looking for you". This particular section of Mark's story ends with Jesus moving on to visit other towns and villages as well. But his work was the same: "he travelled all over Galilee, preaching in the synagogues and driving out demons" (Mark 1:39).

Jerusalem. An orthodox Jew sounds the shofar.

MOVING ON

Mark regularly uses such short summary statements to join together the individual stories out of which he constructed his narrative, and they were probably intended as indefinite statements to indicate the general character of Jesus' work, rather than referring to specific occasions. It is certainly striking that if Jesus did in fact travel "all over Galilee", then neither Mark nor the other gospel writers chose to tell us much about it. The stories they record all mainly centre on the northern corner of the region, though incidental comments do occasionally imply that Jesus had visited other towns and cities. Chorazin, for example, is condemned for its unresponsive attitude to Jesus, though there is no record of him ever visiting the place (Matthew 11:21). But there is not even a hint that Jesus ever went to any of the major centres of population such as Sepphoris (only 6 kilometres from Nazareth) or Tiberias (only 10 kilometres from Capernaum).

The most likely explanation for this is that the gospel writers were all constructing selective accounts of Jesus' life and teaching, rather than aiming to document everything that he did. In any event, Mark's narrative soon brings Jesus back to his home base in Capernaum. This time he did not need to go out to find a crowd: they came to him, and surrounded his house. Here too, the twin themes of words and deeds are central to what happened. For while Jesus was teaching, a man with some kind of paralysis was lowered through the roof, still stretched out on his bed, and deposited at the feet of Jesus. This would not be as difficult as it sounds, for the single storey house would have a flat roof constructed of poles laid across the tops of the walls, with

branches spread over them, and then the whole lot covered with mud. Houses of this type can still be seen in the Muslim Quarter of the old city of Jerusalem. Mark's main concern, however, is not with these details but with what then happened to the man: he was healed! But a new element comes into this story. For Jesus not only healed the man: he also announced that, because of the great faith of the friends who had brought him, his sins were forgiven too (Mark 2:1-12).

OUT AND ABOUT

Only a minority of stories show Jesus speaking with large crowds, either in synagogues or homes. Most of his time was spent out of

WHO WERE THE DISCIPLES?

The Jewish Mishnah sets three objectives for rabbis: "Be deliberate in judgement, raise up many disciples, and make a fence around the Law" (Aboth 1:1ff.). Jesus, of course, was not a typical rabbi. Indeed, this was what many people found so attractive about him. Rabbis were trained to repeat the teachings of their own teacher, whereas Jesus was bold enough to say new things – and frequently did so to the discomfort of the conventional religious authorities of the day.

At the same time, Jesus must have seemed rather like one of the rabbis. Like them, he certainly had his band of disciples. Trusted friends to whom he handed on his teachings, in the hope and expectation that they would both preserve them and pass them on to future generations. Some experts have assumed that, like the rabbis, Jesus insisted his disciples actually learn his teachings off by heart. There can be no doubt that much of what he said is eminently

memorable. But it is unlikely that Jesus operated this way. Had he done so, we would expect to have just one gospel, instead of the four we now have. The fact that we have more than one account of his life and teaching suggests that Jesus encouraged his disciples to reflect on what he was saying, and to use it creatively rather than repeat it woodenly. At the same time, we can be sure that the disciples – living and working in a Jewish environment with this special reverence for religious traditions – would be careful to ensure that they faithfully preserved the gist of what Jesus had to say.

But who were these disciples? Their names are listed more than once in the New Testament, but apart from the leading lights we know little about them. Those we do know something about were certainly a diversified group of people. Certainly not religious types. The first four to be called – Andrew, Peter, James and

John – were fishermen. The cultured citizens of Jerusalem later branded them "ignorant and uneducated" (Acts 4:13). In reality, they were probably middle-class entrepreneurs. The fact that they were able to leave their fishing to follow Jesus, but then later return to it as a means of livelihood, suggests they were in partnership with others who ran the business for them in their absence.

At least one other disciple was probably quite well off too: Matthew. He was a tax collector at the customs point on the Galilean border near to Capernaum. That would certainly not have endeared him to the Jewish establishment, for it meant he was prepared to be a collaborator with the hated Roman authorities. In view of the track record generally of tax collectors, it probably also meant he was something of a crook, making money for himself as well as his Roman masters.

Judas, the only other disciple to feature prominently in the gospel stories, was certainly no saint either. His most infamous deed was his shameful betrayal of Jesus for a mere doors, in the fields, by the roadsides, and along the shores of Lake Galilee. This was where he delivered some of his most distinctive teaching, performed some of the most striking miracles, and challenged people to follow him in a life of commitment and discipleship.

Everyday features of the natural world frequently provided Jesus with the starting point for a discussion about spiritual values. Even something as innocuous as a walk with his disciples on the sabbath day provoked theological discussion when some of them picked stalks of corn as they went (Mark 2:23-28). The familiar sights and sounds of the area also formed the subject-matter for much of his teaching. The Sermon on the Mount

thirty pieces of silver. But he was probably no stranger to treachery and violence. His name "Iscariot" could mean "a man from Kerioth" (and there was such a place). More probably it is connected to a word meaning "assassin" or "dagger man". Like an otherwise unknown disciple, Simon, Judas was in all probability a Zealot, one of a fanatical bunch of fighters who were determined to drive the Romans out of their land at all costs. It is tempting to suppose that Judas joined Jesus hoping that he would be the kind of Messiah figure who would lead such an anti-Roman conspiracy – and when it became obvious that he would not, he betrayed him.

The gospels of Matthew, Mark, and Luke all contain a list of Jesus' twelve disciples, though the lists are not absolutely identical. But apart from these leading figures, the others are all just names to us. Later Christian tradition preserved stories of who they were and what they did, but the truth is we know nothing at all about any of them. Maybe that is the whole point of these lists: Jesus' disciples were all ordinary people – called by him to do extraordinary things. For one of the greatest mysteries of all time is the way that these nobodies were able to take the message of Jesus and use it to transform the Roman empire within a couple of generations. Looking at them closely merely serves to reinforce how ordinary they all were.

The number twelve was obviously important. No doubt the early Christians saw a parallel between Jesus' twelve special disciples, and the twelve tribes of Israel in the Old Testament. These people may have been specially close to Jesus – perhaps because their personal circumstances allowed them the freedom to spend ordinary working days with him. But they were not his only disciples, and in some respects they were not his most important followers. On one occasion Jesus sent out 72 disciples, and they were certainly not the same people as the twelve (Luke 10:1-12). Then there were lots of women involved in Jesus' ministry. Mary Magdalene appears to have been the leading figure in this group. Her association with Jesus began when she had seven demons cast out of her (Luke 8:2), but from then onwards she went everywhere with Jesus, just as the men did. She was a member of the group who travelled with him from Galilee to Jerusalem, and a witness of the crucifixion. More importantly, along with some other women she was the first to receive news of the resurrection, and to share it with the male disciples. Jesus' close friends and associates clearly included many more than just the twelve male disciples. It was natural for the gospel writers – living as they did in a male-dominated culture – to give prominence to the men around Jesus. The fact that the women made it into the stories at all – often more dedicated and courageous than the men – shows that they too must have been key figures in the group that surrounded Jesus.

describes disciples as "a city built on a hill" (Matthew 5:14), perhaps a reference to Safad or Zefat, north of Tiberias and just off the road to Caesarea Philippi.

One of the earliest parables recorded in the gospels tells the story of a farmer sowing seed on various kinds of soil, and coming to terms with the indifferent plants that generally sprouted up as a result (Mark 4:1-9). The soil in the story ranges from deep and fertile ground to mountainous and barren wastes. It is certainly unlikely that all these types of soil would be concentrated on just one farm, but they could all be found somewhere in Galilee and provided a realistic backdrop for what Jesus wanted to say.

On other occasions, Jesus used the language of fishing to get his message across, describing the careful way that two boats would operate a seine net as a picture of God sorting people out at the final judgment (Matthew 13:47-50). Of course, Jesus also used the imagery of fishing in a more positive way.

Jerusalem viewed from the south west, with the Temple area central and the Kidron Valley and Mount of Olives to the right.

When he called his first disciples, he told them he would teach them to "fish for people" (Mark 1:16-18). In Jewish history, fishing for people had always been bad news. The Old Testament contains vivid descriptions of the inhuman practice of conquerors who took people away with nets and hooks (Amos 4:2, Habakkuk 1:15, Jeremiah 16:16). Many ancient inscriptions show such horrors in graphic detail. But Jesus reversed this, and sent out his disciples to fish for people to give them life, not death.

Jesus obviously felt at home in the natural world. He readily referred to the cycles of nature, and the life of flowers, birds, yeast and fish as images of the way God works. Building on the Jewish belief that God created all things, Jesus had no hesitation in suggesting that God is still at work in the everyday functioning of these natural phenomena.

JESUS' STYLE AS A TEACHER

Modern readers of the gospels can easily imagine Jesus delivering his teaching through extended sermons. Hollywood movies have often characterised him as a somewhat absent-minded visionary, wandering round the countryside talking in an abstract and disconnected way about flowers and birds – imaginative, perhaps, but essentially irrelevant to the realities of everyday life. But the real Jesus was not like this at all. The actual form in which we now have his teaching was constructed by the gospel writers, each of whom wanted to apply it to the concerns and questions of their own readers. Luke (1:1-4) and John (20:30-31, 21:25) both describe this procedure in some detail, and we can see it quite clearly at those points where different gospels use what are obviously the same teachings in different contexts. For example, in Luke 15:1-7, the story of the lost sheep is applied to reaching those who are lost, and bringing them into God's kingdom. But in Matthew 18:12-14, the sheep are those who are already in the kingdom, but in danger of drifting away from it. We can see the same thing when we compare the way Matthew and Luke use the teachings of the Sermon on the Mount. In fact, the "Sermon on the Mount" only features in Matthew (5:1-7:29). Some of the same sayings are collected together in Luke as a "sermon on a level place" (6:17-49), but many more of them appear in totally different contexts in Luke. Matthew in particular seems to be organised topically, with different sections of the gospel homing in on different subjects.

These facts should obviously caution us against being over-confident in supposing we can say too much about Jesus' style as a teacher. But it is striking that the gospels rarely show him delivering what we today would recognise as "sermons". Virtually none of his teaching was in monologue style, in which he spoke and others merely listened. Two-way communication was obviously important for Jesus – and when other people were occasionally reticent to engage in discussion, he often elicited a response by asking them questions. Even where the answers must have been obvious (as on the road to Emmaus, Luke 24:13-32, or at the Pool of Bethesda, John 5:1-10), Jesus was always careful to give people the opportunity to voice their own concerns. When we analyse his style closely, asking questions turns out to be one of his favourite teaching methods. The other was telling stories. The combination of these two things goes a long way towards explaining his success in captivating the imagination of ordinary people. He was certainly different from conventional religious experts. For one thing, he was prepared to listen first to what others might be saying. And by telling stories he avoided giving the impression of having all the answers. His stories could be understood at many different levels, and always left people space to make their own judgments about what he might be getting at.

Capernaum on the shores of Lake Galilee. Jesus first declared his mission in the synagogue here.

A catch of fish from the Sea of Galilee.

WORDS AND DEEDS

"I hear, I forget; I see, I understand; I do, I remember". The words are from an old Chinese proverb. But Jesus was well acquainted with the principle. Words are not usually the most effective form of communication. Much of Jesus' most distinctive teaching was delivered not in words but in actions – and when he spoke, it was often in further explanation of his deeds. When the rock musical *Godspell* characterised Jesus as a clown, it picked up some highly significant elements of his character. Jesus certainly liked having fun, and had a great sense of humour –

MESSIANIC EXPECTATIONS

Was Jesus the Messiah – as he and his followers appear to have claimed – and if he was, what would that mean? This question runs like a golden thread through the entire fabric of the New Testament gospels. The disciples had few hesitations about calling Jesus the Messiah – though they had little idea what it might mean for him to be Messiah. And others, of course, found all such talk either irrelevant or unbelievable. But what exactly were they all arguing about? Who was the Messiah anyway, and what part did this enigmatic figure play in Jewish national life at the time of Jesus? To find some answers to these questions, we need to dig deep into Jewish history and religion.

Dissatisfaction with the way things are seems to be a part of being human. The world is in a mess – but with the right circumstances and opportunities, things may change for the better. Or so people the world over tell themselves – and the Jews were no exception. Over the centuries, they had experienced more than their fair share of oppression and disadvantage, and as Jesus' contemporaries reflected on the state of their nation, there were many things that could obviously be improved. The one thing that brought more anguish than most was the fact that they were not in control of their own national destiny. Their land was not their own, but was ruled and controlled by distant emperors in Rome. Emperors who for the most part had never visited Palestine, nor would they care to do so – but who would never relinquish

this outpost of the empire because of its strategic situation at the eastern end of the Mediterranean Sea.

You could change a few names and places, and that description would be appropriate to most periods of ancient Jewish history. For the greater part of their history, the Jewish people had been subservient to other more powerful nations. The geographical location of Palestine almost guaranteed that the superpowers of the day would always be fighting for possession of it. For centuries, the two major power centres of the Middle East had been, on the one hand Egypt, and on the other Mesopotamia. Even before the emergence of Israel as a nation, Egypt had been overlord to the peoples of Canaan, and continued in this role for much of the early Israelite period. As time passed and Egypt's influence diminished, it was the turn of whoever ruled Mesopotamia to exercise varying degrees of control over Palestine and its smaller nations. First the Assyrians, whose power lasted for 200 years and more, followed by the Babylonians, who in turn were succeeded by the Persians – until eventually in the fourth century BC the Greeks led by Alexander the Great brought Palestine under the control of powers based in southern Europe. On his premature death, Alexander's empire was divided among his generals, whose successors held on to Palestine until the Romans incorporated it into their own vast empire.

People with a lesser sense of their own status might have been prepared

to accept that they were not destined to become one of the great political power centres of the world – and learned to live with the consequences, by accommodating themselves to whichever superpower carried most influence. But the Jewish nation was made of different stuff. Inspired by religious fervour, they found it impossible to accept that they should be a third-rate state, and always aspired to something greater. If they could not rule the whole world, then at least they ought to be in charge of their own land. The reasons for this go back deep into the roots of the Old Testament. At the very start of their national history, their ancestor Abraham had been promised that his descendants would become "a great nation" (Genesis 12:2) – a promise that was renewed to David, one of Israel's greatest kings, when he was told: "You will always have descendants, and [God] will make your kingdom last for ever. Your dynasty will never end" (2 Samuel 7:16). This promise to David encouraged the belief that the kingdom based in Jerusalem, and headed by a member of David's family, would play some central part in the emergence of God's own Kingdom, in which people could live at peace with one another, and in fellowship with God.

At least, that was the theory. But the reality was often different, as one king after another showed himself to be quite unfit, both morally and spiritually, to lead the people in ways that reflected the will of God. As one king succeeded another, there was always the hope that the next occupant of David's throne would be better – less corruptible and more faithful. But from about the time of

A busy street in the old city of Jerusalem. Jesus' disciples came from many different backgrounds.

Isaiah in the eighth century BC, even prophetic visionaries within the nation became increasingly disillusioned with David's family. Each new king was still greeted with enthusiasm, but the nation's hopes for a better future were expressed in ever more idealistic terms. History seemed to show that the actual king in Jerusalem was never going to change things. If the ancient dreams were to come true, it would need to be through an ideal king whom God would send directly to lead the people. When the state of Judah fell to Babylon in 586 BC and both Jerusalem and its temple were destroyed, nationalist hopes were dealt a severe, but not yet fatal, blow. There were still one or two of David's descendants living in exile in Babylon – and when Cyrus the Persian began to allow the exiles to return, renewed hopes were pinned on some of them. These hopes would

THE COMING OF THE MESSIAH

Many Old Testament passages point forward to a great coming person. Jesus himself told the scribes and pharisees that the Old Testament scriptures testified to him (John 5:39), and after his resurrection he explained to two disciples "what was said in all the scriptures concerning himself" (Luke 24:27). The early Christians linked many Old Testament passages directly to the person of Jesus as they explained their faith to others. They were certain that Jesus was the Messiah of whom the Old Testament spoke.

MESSIAH IN THE LINE OF DAVID	2 Samuel 7:8-16	Acts 2:29-36, 1 Corinthians 1:23-4
THE BRANCH OF DAVID'S LINE	Isaiah 11:1	Matthew 1:1
THE SUFFERING SERVANT	Isaiah 52:13–53:12	1 Peter 2:21-5, Mark 10:45
SON OF MAN	Daniel 7:13-4	Matthew 26:64
GOD WITH US, IMMANUEL	Isaiah 7:14	Luke 1:32, Matthew 1:23
BORN IN BETHLEHEM, OF A VIRGIN	Micah 5:2, Isaiah 7:14	John 7:42, Luke 1:31
THE LORD HIMSELF, FOLLOWING THE "HERALD"	Malachi 3:1	Matthew 3:3

soon be dashed, however, as things went from bad to worse – and from then onwards, the Messiah came to be very definitely identified with a supernatural figure sent by God to establish a kingdom of justice and peace.

By the time of Jesus, many people – perhaps the majority – were looking for the Messiah to come very soon. Not that there was any one clear-cut expectation of what this might mean. There was much speculation not only about when the Messiah would come, and what he would do – but even who he would be. The word "Messiah" itself means "anointed one" – a fitting description for a successor to Judah's kings, all of whom were invested in office by being anointed with oil. But in the Old Testament, kings were not the only ones to be anointed. High priests were – and some Jewish groups looked for a Messiah who would be a priest, as well as a kingly figure. Many more expected that Elijah or some other prophetic character from the past would return

first to prepare the way for the Messiah. And just about everyone believed that when the Messiah came, he would destroy all hostile world powers and establish his own glorious kingdom, which would be essentially limited to Israel. Jerusalem would become the centre of the earth, and God would quite literally rule the nations.

When people looked at Jesus, they naturally compared him with their own picture of what the Messiah would be like when he came. With so many diverse views current, it is not surprising that there were many opinions as to whether Jesus could be the one. He certainly had the popular charismatic appeal that could be expected of the Messiah, and people of all sorts found themselves drawn to him. But he seemed either unwilling or unable to do many of the things popularly associated with the Messiah – like fighting the Romans , and re-establishing a Jewish state. And yet he talked about God's Kingdom having come, and of himself as a leading actor in the

drama. No wonder that many people simply did not know what to make of him.

while the visual and experiential were both important aspects of his ministry. Never more strikingly so than in some of the stories we call the miracles.

The healing miracles are so thoroughly integrated into the main storyline of all four gospels that we need not doubt they formed one of the major concerns of Jesus' entire life. Non-Christian writers of the time rarely mention Jesus, but when they do the miracles generally feature in their descriptions of him. Josephus wrote of Jesus as "a wise man" and "a doer of wonderful deeds" (*Antiquities* 18.63-4), while the Babylonian Talmud described him as practising "sorcery" (*Sanhedrin* 43a). The healing miracles, however, are only one aspect of the miraculous deeds of Jesus. Even more striking in some respects are the "nature miracles" – those stories in which Jesus interacts not with other people, but with the natural world. Stories like the feeding of the five thousand (Mark 6:30-44), the four thousand (Mark 8:1-10), the stilling of the storm (Mark 4:35-41), or walking on the water (Mark 6:45-52) all come under this heading.

JESUS' LIFESTYLE

Most people have a mental image of who Jesus was, and what he looked like. Down the centuries, artists have depicted him looking much like their own heroes. Medieval European artists drew him with the features of their own patrons. Modern Christians often like to think of him as poor and marginalised – one of the oppressed classes, maybe homeless, quite possibly unemployed, and certainly pushed out to the fringes of society by hostile establishment figures. A non-person with whom those in similar circumstances today can readily identify. But what was Jesus really like? Perhaps we shall never truly know for certain – and ultimately it may not matter, for Jesus' teachings will inevitably take

on fresh nuances as people from different social experiences reflect on his meaning for them. Nevertheless, the gospels do give us some clues to Jesus' own economic and cultural circumstances.

Romantic Christmas card images of his birth often emphasise the apparent poverty of Jesus' family. Mary and Joseph were so poor they were unable to afford a place to stay in Bethlehem – even at a time of enormous personal need. Most parents would make a special effort at a time like this, so if Mary ended up giving birth in a stable, they must have been extremely poor. But the true situation cannot have been so simple. Whatever the explanation for their unusual lodging place, Mary

and Joseph are unlikely to have been there for purely financial reasons. Joseph is described as a "carpenter" (Mark 6:3), though the actual Greek word used in the gospels really means a general builder, rather than a worker exclusively in wood. The natural conclusion would be that Joseph had his own business in Nazareth, and would therefore be at least among the middle classes of such a place. Artists' impressions of Jesus working as a young man in a thriving family concern are probably not far off the mark. The fact that Jesus received some education – as we know from his ability to read the Hebrew scriptures in the synagogue – also points in the same direction. And it is perhaps not altogether coincidental that his first disciples were fishermen, who were also engaged in running their own family

businesses. Perhaps Jesus had known them in some commercial capacity before he began his own ministry.

When Jesus was growing up, Galilee was a prosperous place to live, and it is tempting to associate the development of his own life with the movements of political and economic fortunes in the immediate vicinity of Nazareth. Though it is never mentioned in the gospels, one of the largest cities in Galilee was located only 7 or 8 kilometres north of Nazareth. This was the city of Sepphoris – a place with a long history, and historic connections with the nationalism that often bubbled just beneath the surface of Jewish culture. After the death of Herod the Great, Sepphoris had been the scene of concerted opposition to Roman rule, and it was only stifled when the Roman general Varus

burned the city and took many of its people away into slavery. But it was not long before Herod Antipas rebuilt it as an essentially Gentile and pagan city, and chose it as his capital. Out of a total Galilean population of about 350,000, as many as 40,000 might have lived in Sepphoris. During the years when Jesus was a teenager, much reconstruction work was taking place there, and it is hard to imagine that, as a local builder in a nearby village, Jesus and his family would not have been involved in it.

With a city of that size literally just over the horizon from Nazareth, it is equally hard to believe that Jesus was totally isolated from the great urban culture of the Roman world. In fact, Sepphoris had a striking theatre at which the plays of Greek and Roman writers were regularly performed. For all the same reasons,

it is highly likely that Jesus would be able to speak Greek, which was the official language of the empire and was certainly used in places like Sepphoris – though no doubt Jewish people continued to use Aramaic in their own family circles. When we place Jesus in this context, we can reasonably conclude that, far from being an unsophisticated country boy, he was actually well informed about Hellenistic culture – and could speak at least three languages, if not four (Greek, Aramaic, Hebrew, and maybe Latin).

In AD 25, the local economy suffered a severe setback, when the centre of government was moved away from Sepphoris to Tiberias. Many people must have seen their livelihood disappear overnight and as a result, many would be thrown out of work. Perhaps Jesus and his family

The Old Testament had frequently described God's coming Kingdom as a time when the whole environment would be put right, and hostility between humankind and the natural world would disappear. Through the healings, Jesus was declaring that God had empowered him to change for the better the lives of people. In the nature miracles, he affirmed that God cares for the physical environment as well. We can see the relationship of these themes in the feeding of the five thousand (Mark 6:30-44), the stilling of the storm (Mark 4:35-41), and the healing of a demon-possessed man (Mark 5:1-20).

Nowadays, pilgrims celebrate the miraculous feeding with the loaves and fishes at et-Tabgha, an ancient Greek settlement just south of Capernaum. The fourth century nun Egeria identified this as the place, though in reality it is difficult to say where it happened. John locates it on the "other" side of the lake, which usually means the eastern side for him. But Mark seems to place it on the west side, somewhere near Capernaum, while Luke

The Pool of Bethesda in Jerusalem: the scene of one of Jesus' miracles.

were among them – not to mention some of his first disciples. Is it just coincidence that he began his public ministry not long afterwards, and that there seem to have been many people with nothing to do all day but listen to him and follow him around?

All the gospels depict Jesus as a wandering teacher and healer. There were many such people around at the time. His appearance and lifestyle were not all that unusual. If they had been, people would have been less than eager to listen to him – and he would certainly never have had the chance to speak in the synagogue, or be invited into the homes of leading members of the community. Yet he apparently had ready access not only to business people such as Peter and John, but to tax-gatherers like Levi, synagogue leaders like Jairus, and Pharisees (at least one of whom

invited him to his home, Luke 7:36-50), not to mention other community leaders such as Joseph of Arimathea or Nicodemus, and people like Roman centurions. Taking clues from statements such as "the Son of Man has nowhere to lay his head" (Matthew 8:20), some interpreters have seen Jesus and his disciples as a trendy band of homeless drop-outs, a bit like the hippy movement of the 1960s. But Jesus often used deliberate exaggeration to get his points across. In other places, he talks about people having planks of wood in their eyes, or of needing to cut their hands off or pull their eyes out. Statements about being homeless and rootless were also probably made for their dramatic effect. We can be quite sure that if Jesus had been no more than a flashy eccentric, people like the Pharisees would hardly have

bothered to take him seriously. A more careful reading of the gospels suggests that he had a regular home base in Capernaum – either belonging to himself, or to one of his friends. Some (though not all) of his disciples must have been reasonably well off. And he also enjoyed the support of a group of fairly wealthy female sponsors, including one "Joanna, whose husband Chuza was an officer in Herod's court" (Luke 8:3).

locates the miracle somewhere near Bethsaida.

The precise location does not matter, for there is no doubt about its meaning. The story is about power. Mark describes this event just after the disgusting story of how John the Baptist's head was served up on a plate to satisfy the ghoulish appetite of the Herod family. It might seem as if the power belongs to the drunken debauchery of such royal feasts. But real power is to be found with Jesus, feeding the crowd on broken bread and fishes on a lonely hillside. Jewish tradition had thought of the feeding of hungry people as one of the signs that the messianic age was dawning (Isaiah 25:6-9). And the crowd out on the hillside recognised this – though few if any of them realised that spiritual power is not necessarily the same thing as military might. Indeed, the way Mark describes the people sitting down "in rows, in groups of a hundred and groups of fifty" (Mark 6:40) sounds

Early evening. The setting sun reflected in the waters of the Sea of Galilee.

rather like the organisation of Old Testament armies. Perhaps these men were attracted to Jesus because they saw in him a possible

CITIES THAT JESUS VISITED

■ CAPERNAUM

In the time of Jesus, Capernaum was probably quite a prosperous town, though not particularly large (it may have been no more than about 800 by 250 metres in area). But it had a strong economy, supported mainly by fishing and agriculture – and it occupied a strategic position on the northern border of Galilee. This ensured it had a Roman military garrison with its own centurion, as well as a customs post to regulate traffic crossing the border.

Jesus seems to have settled in Capernaum quite early in his ministry, and it became in effect his home base for all his work in Galilee. Peter's home was also in

Capernaum, and its site is commemorated today by an octagonal church with what is believed to be the "house of Peter" beneath it. The town has been extensively excavated by modern archaeologists, and we have a good idea what a typical home here would look like. The natural stone of the region is a distinctive black basalt, and this formed the foundations of the houses, as well as the building materials for the walls, all held together with a mortar made from local mud. This made a functional structure, though it would not be strong enough to support an upper storey, and the flat roof laid across the top of the walls would need to be quite light in weight. Inside, the

floors would be paved with the same rough basalt rock.

■ MAGDALA

This was another town on the western side of the Sea of Galilee, just south of Capernaum and about midway between there and Tiberias . Its Hebrew name had been Migdal, which means a tower, so presumably there had been some kind of fortress there. But Josephus uses its Greek name, Tarichea – a word which describes it perfectly, for it means a factory for pickling and salting fish. In the time of Jesus it had an enviable reputation as a fish processing centre – and its products were highly prized, even being exported as far as Spain. It was the home town of Mary Magdalene, one messianic leader, to take them into battle against the hated Romans. If they were, that would explain why Jesus was forced to send the disciples off across the lake rather urgently, while he stayed behind to dismiss the crowd himself. Mark does not indicate the reason for this, but the account in John backs up such speculation: "Jesus knew they were about to come and seize him in order to make him king by force ..." (Mark 6:45, John 6:15).

Not surprisingly, the Sea of Galilee plays a significant part in several stories. One of the most striking tells how Jesus and the disciples were crossing the water in a fierce storm. Jesus was asleep in the boat, apparently indifferent to the possibility of a shipwreck. Though they were experienced fishermen, his disciples did not share his confidence, but when they woke him, he simply calmed the storm down. Or, to be more precise, he "rebuked" the wind and the waves – in much the same way as he "rebuked" demons in other stories (Mark 4:35-41). For Jewish people, this would be appropriate language to use. They had

of Jesus' closest followers, and it is often thought that Jesus may have met his first disciples somewhere near here.

■ **TIBERIAS**

This was a completely new city built on the western shore of Galilee by Herod Antipas. When it was finished, in about AD 25, he transferred his entire state organisation to Tiberias from Sepphoris. It was a grand place, with a theatre, stadium, palace – and a big synagogue. There were many fine buildings, with mosaic floors often incorporating Hellenistic art forms. At first, conservative Jews would have nothing to do with it, as it was built on the site of an ancient cemetery. But later it became a great centre of Rabbinic learning, and one

of the four holy cities of Palestine. Many famous rabbis were buried there, including Aqiba, perhaps the greatest of them all. Today, Tiberias is a modern Israeli city, with many natural attractions as a holiday resort. The hot springs just south of the town were there in New Testament times, and were no doubt used then by the rich and famous, just as they are today. Quite possibly they were also used for healing, as similar springs often were elsewhere in the Roman empire. Modern pilgrims may not find healing here. But they can enjoy a dish that was certainly not available in Jesus' time: the delicious "St Peter's Fish" (*Tipalia galilaea*).

Tiberias is mentioned in the gospels only briefly: in a reference to boats coming from here and then sailing to Capernaum after the

feeding of the five thousand (John 6:23). But Herod Antipas is mentioned several times in the gospels, in connection with John the Baptist. He also features in the stories of Jesus' trials, as the Galilean Herod who concluded Jesus was a harmless eccentric.

■ **BETHSAIDA**

This town was not really a part of Galilee, as it was just on the eastern shore of the Lake, beyond the point where the river Jordan comes down from the north. This other side was mostly non-Jewish, but there were some Jews living there, and it would not be unusual to think of it as part of Galilee. Some documents refer to it as Bethsaida Julias, a town that was partly rebuilt by Herod Philip,

The valley between Cana and Nazareth was a route that Jesus would have been familiar with.

and given its new name in honour of Julia, daughter of the emperor Augustus. Bethsaida seems to have been the original home of Philip, Andrew, and Peter (John 1:44, 12:21) – but its inhabitants were unreceptive to the message of Jesus, and he included it with several places that had rejected his teaching (Matthew 11:21).

■ DECAPOLIS

Decapolis was not the name of a city, but of a whole area that extended from the eastern side of the Sea of Galilee, down to the south. Its name means 'ten cities', and these

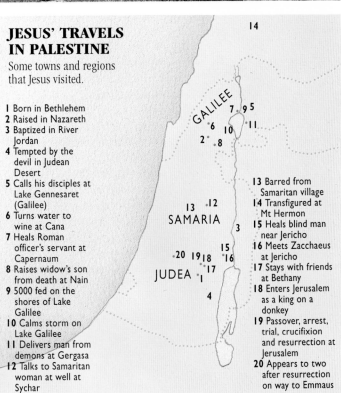

JESUS' TRAVELS IN PALESTINE

Some towns and regions that Jesus visited.

1 Born in Bethlehem
2 Raised in Nazareth
3 Baptized in River Jordan
4 Tempted by the devil in Judean Desert
5 Calls his disciples at Lake Gennesaret (Galilee)
6 Turns water to wine at Cana
7 Heals Roman officer's servant at Capernaum
8 Raises widow's son from death at Nain
9 5000 fed on the shores of Lake Galilee
10 Calms storm on Lake Galilee
11 Delivers man from demons at Gergasa
12 Talks to Samaritan woman at well at Sychar
13 Barred from Samaritan village
14 Transfigured at Mt Hermon
15 Heals blind man near Jericho
16 Meets Zacchaeus at Jericho
17 Stays with friends at Bethany
18 Enters Jerusalem as a king on a donkey
19 Passover, arrest, trial, crucifixion and resurrection at Jerusalem
20 Appears to two after resurrection on way to Emmaus

never been great seafarers – fearing that the sea was not merely hostile, but was the abode of evil spirits and demons. Later Christians faced with fierce persecution by the Roman authorities often used the same images, portraying the church as a ship, tossed around on the sea of hostility and persecution. So Mark's first readers, persecuted for their faith in Nero's Rome, would read here a special message for themselves: with Jesus on board, they could expect to survive, for his power extended even to the most powerful strongholds of evil itself.

The story that follows in Mark dramatically underlines all that. This time, the main character is a man called 'Legion' – so named because he has a "legion" of demons in him. He was clearly in a distressed state (there were 6000 men in a Roman legion). An outcast from normal life, he lived on the eastern (non-Jewish) side of the Sea of Galilee, existing as best he could in a graveyard. The man was eager to meet Jesus, and ran up to him as soon as he landed. In response to his obvious desire to be freed from this demonic oppression, Jesus allowed the demons to escape into

settlements were apparently founded in the years following the death of Alexander the Great by his successors. They were Greek cities, transplanted into Palestine – and were never accepted by nationalist Jews, as their populations were largely Gentile, and entirely supportive of Rome. Such people of mixed Jewish ancestry as did live in the region often ignored much of the Jewish laws and customs. Jesus met the man called Legion in this area, and the fact that pigs were being kept was precisely the sort of custom that antagonised traditional Jewish sensitivities. This man's home was in Gadara, one of the most northerly of the ten cities, and whose territory probably included part of the shore of Galilee as shipping seems to have formed a large part of its commercial operations.

■ CAESAREA PHILIPPI

At 350 metres above sea level, Caesarea Philippi must have been one of the highest places Jesus ever visited. Standing in the foothills of Mount Hermon, it is well to the north of the Sea of Galilee, and was in the territory of Herod Philip. From ancient times it had been a place of special pilgrimage. Water and fertility gods were worshipped there in antiquity, and the Greeks dedicated a cave which contained one of the sources of the Jordan to Pan and the nymphs. They called this cave the Paneion, and the town Paneas. Augustus gave it to Herod the Great, who built a large white marble temple there, and dedicated it to the emperor. Philip then ruled it until AD 34, extending it and naming it in honour of the emperor Tiberius and

himself. It later passed into the hands of Herod Agrippa II. Its population was almost entirely non-Jewish and pagan – a particularly appropriate place for Peter to declare that Jesus was the Messiah of the one true God.

some pigs feeding nearby. The power of the disorder which had afflicted the man was all too obvious, as it took 2000 pigs to contain all these demons. But the last laugh was on them, as the pigs immediately ran over a cliff and plunged into the sea – over which Jesus had already asserted his absolute authority!

The man wanted to join up with Jesus, but instead he was sent off to share the good news with his own people back home. Throughout his work in Galilee, Jesus had to handle an uneasy tension between wanting to alert people to the important role he felt he had in God's ultimate plans, while deterring them from wrong understandings that would project him as an exclusively political figure. As a result, Jesus regularly told those he healed not to speak openly about him. But in this instance, there was no such need for caution – probably because the man was a citizen of the Decapolis, and he was unlikely to come into contact with Jewish leaders there.

FAITH AND UNCERTAINTY

Even those who were wholeheartedly committed to Jesus still had many questions about him. Peter's story is typical. Fired by enthusiasm when he met Jesus on the shore of Galilee, he nevertheless took some considerable time to sort out his own feelings and attitudes towards Jesus. How could he be the Messiah, when he seemed so different from traditional expectations? And what was he actually asking his disciples to do and believe? It is perhaps significant that Jesus took his followers away on a retreat to the remote territory around Caesarea Philippi, before he asked them the crucial question: Who do you think I am? It was Peter who was bold enough to attempt some sort of answer: "You are the Messiah" (Mark 8:29, Luke 9:20) and, according to Matthew, "the Son of the living God" (Matthew 16:16). It is not accidental that the next paragraph in all three synoptic gospels shows Jesus warning the disciples that messiahship for him did not mean what they thought – and hoped – it meant. That far from being a conquering warrior, he would fulfil his vocation through suffering and death. Something that even Peter was unable to comprehend.

But if "the medium is the message", then there was no

doubting that Jesus was putting across a radical new understanding of messiahship and salvation. He himself was the "wrong" kind of person, born in unpromising circumstances. He was neither rich nor powerful.

He consistently identified himself not with heroes, but with ordinary people. He did not eat in the palaces of the rich and famous, but with unemployed people on remote hillsides – or at their homely wedding feasts (the scene of one of his miracles, John 2:1-12). He shared the sorrows and joys of people who were nobodies, and for his disciples he chose a rag-bag of people from many different walks of life. It was not essential to be poor and homeless to follow him, but all those who were attracted by his message shared his radical commitment to discovering and doing God's will. They empathised with his vision of weak people who could change the world. They resonated with the idea that the last could become first, and the vulnerable and powerless could yet be great in God's kingdom. It was often a struggle for them to come to terms with what Jesus' teachings might mean in everyday life. But they knew he spoke their language, and they were ready to trust him.

3

INCREASING CONFLICTS

MANY PEOPLE found that Jesus' message addressed their concerns in a unique way. In addition to the small group of committed disciples, large crowds also followed Jesus wherever he went, desperate to hear what he had to say. Yet in spite of his obvious popularity, Jesus was not everyone's favourite spiritual teacher. Others found his message theologically unacceptable and personally threatening. Since he was so uncompromising in his claims, it was inevitable that mere disagreement should turn to outright and ultimately violent opposition.

JESUS AND HIS FRIENDS

The first time Mark mentions such opposition, Jesus was at a party (Mark 2:13-17). All the gospels depict Jesus as a sociable person. One of the first stories in John's gospel shows Jesus at a party – this time a wedding feast, where the wine ran out, and Jesus produced some more out of water, apparently for no other reason

Cana, scene of Jesus' first miracle at a wedding feast.

than to help the festivities along (John 2:1-10). He obviously enjoyed the company of other people, even though it earned him a slightly dubious reputation as "a glutton and a drinker, a friend of tax collectors and other outcasts" (Matthew 11:19). The particular gathering highlighted by Mark took place in the home of Levi, shortly after Jesus had invited him to be one of his disciples. No doubt it was a celebration meal, at which Levi introduced Jesus to his other friends. It takes only a little imagination to guess who they were. For Levi himself was a tax collector. Tax collectors were not economically deprived – quite the opposite – but they were not popular characters in first century Palestine. If they had any friends at all there was a good chance they would be criminals and outcasts of various sorts.

The Romans never directly collected taxes themselves: in outposts of the empire, they had too few personnel for that sort of thing. Instead, they sold the right to collect taxes to the highest bidders. Once these local entrepreneurs had gathered what they needed to fulfil the terms of their contracts with the Romans, then

THE RELIGIOUS BACKGROUND TO THE STORIES OF JESUS

In his book *The Jewish War*, the historian Josephus observes that "Jewish philosophy takes three forms. The followers of the first school are called Pharisees, of the second Sadducees, and the third sect, which has a reputation for being more disciplined, is the Essenes" (*Jewish War* 2.119-120). He also identifies a fourth group, the Zealots, who were evidently distinctive enough, though are not listed as a "philosophical" group. Josephus was writing for educated Greeks and Romans, which no doubt explains why he talks of "philosophy" rather than religion. Most Romans had no time for Jewish religion, regarding it as primitive

and unsophisticated. But they always wanted to know about somebody else's philosophy.

Three of these groups feature in the gospel stories. Two of them – Pharisees and Sadducees – play a prominent part (along with Scribes), while the Zealots are only mentioned briefly, and the Essenes do not feature at all. All these groups originated in the two centuries preceding the birth of Christ, and their actual membership was probably quite small. But one way and another, their influence extended throughout much of the community. Their status can usefully be compared with political parties in

today's world. Their wider following would be much larger than their actual membership. Most people would not formally join such a group, but almost everybody would identify with the ideals of one particular faction.

So far as the Sadducees and Pharisees are concerned, our understanding of them is hampered by the almost total absence of any evidence contemporary with the time of Jesus. There are voluminous rabbinic writings dating from after the fall of Jerusalem in AD 70, and Judaism in the time of Jesus was probably not too different. But we have no hard evidence to that effect, and any conclusions we may reach must therefore always be carefully qualified. A particular problem is that the later texts do not show Judaism as a religion that was prone anything else was personal profit for them. It is no wonder that people were so hostile to them. To faithful Jewish people, it was bad enough that these renegades were prepared to work for the hated Romans at all. But to rob their own people by charging excess taxes – and to do it all perfectly legally – was loathsome in the extreme, offending personal morality as well as certain sections of Old Testament law. The price of economic success as a tax collector was to be treated with contempt by respectable citizens, and classed with other undesirables such as drunkards, prostitutes, and common thieves.

So when Jesus chose to mix freely with characters like this, decent religious people were understandably shocked. In his *Rules of Civility*, US leader George Washington advised, "Associate yourself with men of good quality if you esteem your own reputation; for 'tis better to be alone than in bad company." Jesus' contemporaries shared the same opinion. If he was really a prophet with a message from God, then how could he mix so openly with leaders of the Palestinian underworld? Surely a

to hypocrisy in quite the thoroughgoing way the New Testament seems to suggest. That is not to say there were no self-righteous people in the system – it would indeed be surprising if that were the case – but it does put a different perspective on the sort of criticisms we find in the gospels, and implies they must have been directed to specific individuals rather than being a general condemnation of the whole of Jewish spirituality.

■ SADDUCEES

In the time of Jesus, the Sadducees were probably quite a small group. But they were very influential. Many of the priests in the Jerusalem temple would be

Sadducees, along with other well-to-do classes of Jewish society. Their origins are unclear. Linguistically,

the name "Sadducee" seems to mean "son of Zadok", though historians have been unable to trace their origins back to any particular individual of that name. Others suggest that the term comes from a Hebrew word, *sadiq*, meaning "moral integrity", or "righteousness", while yet others relate it to the Greek word *syndicoi*, meaning "members of the council". The Sadducees were indeed members of the Jewish council of seventy (the Sanhedrin). And they

The Chi-Rho was a "secret sign" used by the early Christians, made of the first two letters of the name of Christ in Greek.

religious teacher ought to give priority to decent people living honourable lives, and making a conscious effort to obey the law? Yet Jesus apparently dismissed such criticisms: "People who are well do not need a doctor, but only those who are sick. I have not come to call respectable people, but outcasts" (Mark 2:17).

UNDERSTANDING THE OPPOSITION

The "respectable people" to whom Jesus refers are usually called "scribes and Pharisees" by the gospel writers. They – together with the Sadducees – were Jesus' typical opponents. Of course they were not his only adversaries, nor should we imagine that every single scribe, Pharisee and Sadducee was implacably opposed to all that Jesus stood for. Several gospel stories show such people seeking Jesus out to ask genuine questions, including

A Sephardic Jew with phylactery and shawl.

were extreme conservatives.

In terms of religious belief, the Sadducees took as their supreme authority the Law given to Moses and contained in the first five books of the Old Testament. By rejecting other parts of the Hebrew scriptures, they also found themselves unable to accept beliefs that had developed at later stages in Israelite history – things like life after death, a final judgment, or a future resurrection. They may theoretically have believed in the coming of a Messiah, but this seems to have had little impact on their way of life. Sadducees were not unwilling to collaborate with the Roman forces of occupation, at least when they believed that co-operation would allow the Jewish people to preserve some influence over their national life.

one who welcomed him to a meal at his home (Luke 7:36-50), while at least two members of the religious establishment (Nicodemus and Joseph of Arimathea) seem to have accepted his teaching.

Modern readers of the gospel stories might be forgiven for supposing that these people were personally responsible for all that was corrupt in Jewish society, and that Judaism (especially in its Pharisaic form) was so far removed from the original intentions of the Old Testament faith that Jesus would of necessity be in conflict with it. That is how it sometimes looked to the Christians for whom the gospels were written later in the first century. In cities like Rome and Ephesus – not to mention Jerusalem and Antioch – the Jewish communities often went out of their way to make life difficult for the church. It is not hard to understand the historical and sociological reasons for such antagonism. But theologically, things were not that simple. Most Jewish believers had a strong personal trust in God, and tried to keep the Old Testament Law as part of their faith response to what

■ PHARISEES

In everyday affairs, the Sadducees found it necessary to work along with the Pharisees. The Sanhedrin had members from both groups, but in the country at large the Pharisees were probably a much bigger group than the Sadducees. Josephus suggests there were as many as 6000 of them in Jesus' time. Many Pharisees were also "scribes" – professional lawyers and students of the Old Testament. These people were not paid for serving on the Sanhedrin, and in theory they were supposed to give their religious teachings free of charge, though in practice they probably received payment (Mark 12:40). But the ideal was for such a teacher to work at an ordinary occupation as well as studying the Old Testament Law.

Because there was no such thing as a "professional Pharisee", members of the group were drawn from a broad cross-section of the community. What held them together was not social class as such, but their common allegiance to the Law and its interpretation, though inevitably the strong demarcation between devout believers and "people of the land" led to a form of social stratification. As well as people of private means, many ordinary working people would also be Pharisees – people, perhaps, like some of Jesus' own relatives. Structurally, they were a national organisation, with many local groups in towns and villages throughout Palestine.

The Pharisees shared the Sadducees' reverence for the Old Testament – though they accepted all of it as authoritative, not just the

first five books. They also realised, however, that their way of life had changed a lot since the Old Testament was first written. To be relevant to new circumstances, it needed to be given fresh interpretations. Even apparently simple statements such as the Ten Commandments needed to be refined and applied specifically to the sort of challenges faced by ordinary people in everyday situations.

To achieve this praiseworthy aim, and give specific practical guidance on the meaning of their scriptures, the Pharisees set out many subsidiary rules and regulations. The intention was to "make a fence for the Law", as the opening words of the *Pirke Aboth* ("teachings of the fathers") puts it. This meant, in effect, surrounding the law by so many secondary rules that no one was ever

God had done in the life of their nation. They were not legalists, trying to blackmail God by their own moral goodness. On the contrary, they were honest and straightforward people – and intensely devout.

Jesus himself was apparently quite happy to share in the worship of local synagogues on a regular basis – something he would presumably not have done had he been fundamentally disillusioned with what went on there. In his teaching, he accepted

A Moroccan Jewess watches the Bar Mitzvah ceremony over the partition at the Western Wall in Jerusalem.

likely to get within reach of breaking the actual God-given law itself. It was these secondary rules that Jesus found most offensive – though most Pharisees did actually succeed in keeping them. Josephus does not identify Pharisees as a group as hypocrites. On the contrary, he reports how "the people of the cities hold them in the highest esteem, because they both preach and practise the very highest moral ideas" (*Antiquities* 18.11).

The Pharisees had other distinctive views. Unlike the Sadducees they had no difficulty believing in a future life, ultimate judgment, and an overarching purpose behind history. They probably shared the general messianic fervour of their day, and though they would not have instigated any form of revolt they covertly supported some of those who did.

All that remains of the settlement of the Essene community at Qumran.

■ ZEALOTS

The Zealots were in effect the undercover military arm of the Pharisees. Religiously, they certainly shared the Pharisaic outlook. But, in Josephus's words, "they have an insatiable passion for liberty; and they are convinced that God alone is to be their only master and lord ... no fear can compel them to give this title to anyone else ..." (*Antiquities* 18.11). Josephus called them a "philosophical sect", but the Zealots were more concerned with politics than religion. Not that the two could easily be separated in first century Palestine, of course.

They originated with a Galilean called Judas, who led a revolt against the Romans in the early years of the first century AD. But their spiritual and ideological roots can be traced a lot further back than that. They were heirs to the tradition of guerilla warfare pioneered by the Maccabees when the Jewish national heritage came under serious threat from the Greek king Antiochus IV. Against all

the odds, the Maccabees defeated his well equipped forces, and popular nostalgia saw them as a model of what could be accomplished by men fired only with zeal for their religious cause. A disciple called Simon is identified as a Zealot in Mark 3:18. Judas Iscariot may also have been one, as was Barabbas, the robber released instead of Jesus (Mark 15:6-15).

People who were not brave enough to join them still admired the Zealots and would give them whatever assistance and protection they could. Eventually, their subversive activities provoked the war of AD 66-70 which culminated with the occupation of Jerusalem by the Romans, and the destruction of the temple.

■ ESSENES

The Essenes were a different group altogether, and would probably never have been connected to the ministry of Jesus had it not been for one thing: the discovery of the Dead Sea Scrolls shortly after the end of the Second World War. These Scrolls included ancient copies of the Hebrew scriptures, as well as the rules of a monastic community living at Qumran, on the shores of the Dead Sea. They were past their heyday by the time of Jesus, but the monastery was still occupied, and remained so until AD 68.

The Scrolls were first discovered almost fifty years ago, but many are still unpublished, and inaccessible to all but a few scholars. Debate still continues about the people who wrote them. It is hard to know for certain just how important they were in the overall context of first century Palestine. It is easy for us to assume that their influence was everywhere.

the authority of the Old Testament scriptures, and used terms that were part and parcel of the traditional Jewish heritage. Sometimes he wanted to reinterpret such things – as when he linked together the originally separate concepts of Son of Man and Messiah; or when he took the Passover and subtly changed its significance in the Last Supper with his disciples. But he always insisted that his way of looking at things was not a deviation, but the true fulfilment of Jewish hopes and aspirations. To have been at all plausible, he must have been speaking the same language as mainstream Judaism.

Nevertheless, for better or for worse, Scribes, Pharisees and Sadducees feature as the people who were most uncomfortable with what Jesus had to say. No doubt some members of these groups were self-righteous, even hypocrites. Most religions (including Christianity) have their share of such individuals. But as their names imply, these people were not one unified group anyway. They were actually three quite separate groupings, and had some far-reaching disagreements among themselves about

The mere fact that we have the texts inclines us to attach great importance to them. But they were discovered by accident, and it is by no means inconceivable that further coincidental discoveries in the future could radically affect our understanding of the total situation. We must therefore beware of losing a sense of perspective, and concluding that because the Scrolls are important to us, their writers must have dominated the religious scene in the time of Jesus.

The Qumran community were probably a group of Essenes – people also mentioned by Josephus, the Roman author Pliny, and the Alexandrian Jew Philo. In the aftermath of the Maccabean struggle, they had withdrawn from mainstream life, disenchanted with the corruption of the priesthood and temple. Their community became a haven where they could preserve the ancient traditions of religious and moral purity, and prepare themselves to take over the institutions of national life when the opportunity came. On the basis of their reading of the ancient prophecies, they believed that would be very soon.

In the meantime the community lived in a constant state of readiness, engaging in complex ritual washings and scrupulous observance of the Old Testament's food laws. Some have speculated that either John the Baptist or Jesus may have had some connection with this group. But this is unlikely. The Essenes regarded even the Pharisees as dangerous liberals, so they can have had virtually nothing in common with Jesus. What the Dead Sea Scrolls have done is to give us an insight into the mindset of sectarian Judaism at the time. Josephus mentions Essenes who "occupy no one city, but settle in large numbers in every town" (*Jewish War* 2.124). Some of them certainly lived in Damascus, for a document found there is identical with one of the Dead Sea Scrolls. People like this would have found plenty to interest them in Jesus' teaching. For their documents show that they too were looking for the soon arrival of God's Kingdom – the very thing that Jesus claimed to be inaugurating.

religious issues, quite apart from whatever they found
unacceptable about Jesus. Jesus seems to have singled out the
Pharisees for special criticism, and he certainly attacked them in
strong language. So what was wrong with them? Pharisaism at its
best led to intense personal piety, and the teachings of many of
the great rabbis were not altogether out of harmony with Jesus'
own teaching. They had made a special study of the Old Testament
and they were people of integrity, trying as best they could to
preserve the ancient laws God had given to their people. But it
was not so much their beliefs as their personal attitudes that Jesus
condemned. As Jesus experienced them, the Pharisees seemed to
have fallen into an error that is common among religious people.
Whatever their theology said, in practice they behaved as if the
only people who could ever know God were members of their
own organisation. This is why the idea of a God who had a special
concern for the marginalised and the outcast was so baffling, and
why Jesus so often focused on asking who had real spiritual
power: those who were in control of systems and structures, or
those who were powerless. Even so, some things about Jesus were
more objectionable than others, and the conflicts centred on
three particular aspects of his life and teachings.

PERSONAL CHARISMA AND POPULARITY

To put it simply, Jesus was more appealing than many of the other
religious leaders of his day. The Pharisees were bookish people,
who were most at ease in academic debates and controversies.
Jesus was certainly not ignorant: he could hold his own in a
discussion with them. But he was unashamedly a populariser. He
had no difficulty attracting quite substantial crowds wherever he
went. Then, as now, much religious teaching was dull and lifeless.
It was too complex for ordinary people to comprehend, and in
any case often centred on questions that very few people (apart
from religious experts) had ever thought of asking.

The rabbis usually taught their followers to repeat their own
teachings off by heart. There was a good reason for this: a sincere
desire not to corrupt the word of God. By repeating it word for
word, the chance of such corruption was reduced if not
eliminated altogether. But that kind of learning can easily become

tedious and uninteresting. By contrast, Jesus spoke simply. He used language that anyone could understand, and instead of engaging in hair-splitting theological debate, he addressed himself to subjects that were of vital relevance for everyday living.

Jesus had no monopoly on lucid explanation, even in first century Judaism. But if the writings of the rabbis are a fair guide to the way they spoke, then their more creative presentations must often have been obscured by the complexities of detailed textual argument – something that most people neither understood nor cared for. Jesus' teaching, by contrast, was immediate and direct, which is why it captivated people's imagination. For example, most rabbis would not have been unhappy when Jesus described God as King of the coming Kingdom. They themselves occasionally addressed God as "our father, our king" – though they usually also insisted on debating exactly what words like that could mean. But

Looking across the city of Jerusalem towards the Mount of Olives.

Jewish ceremony at the Western Wall in Jerusalem, with the Torah central.

when Jesus taught his followers to pray, he cut through all that and encouraged them to go ahead and boldly address God in everyday language as "Abba", the family word for "Father". People appreciated that kind of bluntness.

Jesus' teaching was never just directed to people's thinking processes. What Jesus said was complemented by what Jesus did, and who he was. Speaking and doing went hand in hand. Quite often, he acted first and spoke afterwards. The miracles are a central part of his message, and are usually (if at all) explained in words only after they have taken place. By addressing his teaching and healing to ordinary people, Jesus naturally enhanced his popularity. But the fact that he was relatively unconventional was bound to make the religious establishment suspicious, if not initially hostile.

TRADITION

It is always dangerous to challenge traditional ways of thinking and behaving. Mavericks can be tolerated for as long as they keep their eccentricities to themselves. But when they imply that there is something fundamentally flawed in the way other people live – and especially when they begin to challenge the system – then they can only expect trouble. This is exactly what happened with Jesus. If mixing with all the "wrong" sort of people had been merely an isolated idiosyncrasy, he might have got away with it. Instead he made his behaviour into a matter of principle. And since in his day social distinctions were inextricably bound up with religious affairs, a person's friends could tell you a lot about his theology.

By the time of Jesus, the old Jewish Law had been supplemented by many rules and regulations, mostly aimed at

A potter at work in the market.

updating and applying an ancient code of conduct to the changed circumstances of a much later generation. In the process, the degree to which a person observed these rules became a method of social stratification within the community. Those who were scrupulous in keeping all the rules wanted little or nothing to do with those who were lax in their observance of the Law. They looked down on them as "people of the land", in effect second class citizens. There was little direct dealing between the two groups, and the more religious people generally despised those whom they considered spiritually corrupt and inferior.

As a result of earlier Jewish history, certain racial and economic tensions were also involved. Samaritans and Galileans were among the leading offenders in this respect. Centuries before, the Samaritans and Jews may have had some common racial ancestry, but by now they were implacably opposed to each other. So far as orthodox Jewish believers were concerned, they were just pagans – claiming that a temple they had built for themselves on Mount Gerizim was of equal status to the temple in Jerusalem! In some respects, they were even worse than pagans, for they had had the chance to accept orthodox Judaism, and had refused. And the Galileans? Well, they were mere opportunists, willing to side with anyone if it was to their advantage. Sociologically, the religious people most opposed to Jesus were probably middle-class town dwellers, who regarded all others as inferior to themselves. When Jesus crossed swords with the cultural establishment in Jerusalem, certain Pharisees dismissed his followers with the comment that "This crowd does not know the Law of Moses, so they are under God's curse!" Adding, for good measure, that "no prophet ever comes from Galilee" (John 7:49, 52). The writings of the rabbis contain similar statements, declaring, for example, that a faithful believer "may not be the guest of one of the people of the land nor may he receive him as a guest in his own raiment" (Desai 2.8-10). In dealing with such sweeping prohibitions and implied condemnation, it is hard to distinguish purely religious considerations from social and racial prejudices.

If this was the way country people were treated by religious town dwellers, then it is no surprise that they were attracted to

JESUS AND THE JEWISH AUTHORITIES

Jerusalem was the centre of Judaism: the centre of the world, according to the rabbis! The temple was there, representing not only Jewish religion but the whole history and heritage of this ancient people. All the gospels are agreed that Jesus spent the last week or so of his life in and around the city, and it was there that he was condemned and crucified. But had he been there before? Apart from a brief childhood visit, the synoptic gospels show Jesus in Jerusalem only in the final week of his life. But Matthew and Luke have a saying which suggests he had been there before: "Jerusalem, Jerusalem! ... How many times have I wanted to put my arms round all your people, just as a hen gathers her chicks under her wings, but you would not let me!" (Matthew 23:37, Luke 13:34). By contrast, John's gospel indicates that Jesus often ministered in Jerusalem during the great pilgrim festivals. Apart from John 2:1-12, 4:3-54, 6:1-71, and 7:1-9, John places the whole of Jesus' ministry in Jerusalem, and specifically mentions three Passovers (2:13, 6:4, 12:1), as well as the Feast of Tabernacles (7:2) and Dedication (10:22).

John is a completely different sort of literature from the other three gospels. Clement of Alexandria explained this difference by reference to the fact that John was believed to be the last gospel to be written, and "seeing that the bare facts were already set forth in the [other] Gospels, on the entreaty of his intimate friends, and inspired by the

Spirit, [he] composed a spiritual Gospel" (quoted in Eusebius, *Ecclesiastical History* VII. vi.14). John's narrative is arranged on a topical or theological basis, more concerned with providing a rounded understanding of the ultimate significance of Jesus' life and teaching than with documenting it in accurate detail. But that does not mean (as was once thought) that John's stories are of no historical value. In fact, recent research has demonstrated beyond any reasonable doubt that John preserves a line of information that is mostly independent of the material used by the other gospel writers, and in some cases its authenticity can be demonstrated. We certainly know that John had accurate knowledge of locations in the city of Jerusalem

prior to its destruction in AD 70. And at several points he provides information that, though different from the synoptic stories, actually complements them in the way we would expect from an independent witness. For instance, at the end of the feeding of the five thousand, Mark tells how Jesus forced his disciples on to a boat and sent them off to the other side of Galilee, while he stayed behind to dismiss the crowds (Mark 6:45). Without repeating the same material, John provides a detailed explanation of why this was appropriate: because the crowd was eager to kidnap him and make him their king (John 6:14-15).

There were three great annual festivals when large numbers of people went on pilgrimage to worship in the temple at Jerusalem.

The Old City of Jerusalem, seen across the Kidron Valley from the Mount of Olives.

At these times, worshippers came not only from Palestine, but from Jewish communities all over the Roman empire. The Festival of Unleavened Bread lasted for a week in March or April, and began with the Passover meal. The one story we have of Jesus' youth takes place during a Passover pilgrimage, when he went with Mary and Joseph (Luke 2:41-52). Then there was also the Festival of Pentecost, seven weeks after that; and the eight day Festival of Tabernacles which was in the autumn, six months after Passover. Each of these commemorated various key events in the history of the nation – events that Jesus was claiming were fulfilled in his own life and ministry.

John wrote his gospel "that you may believe that Jesus is the Messiah, the Son of God, and that through

your faith in him you may have life" (John 20:31), For this purpose, John shows Jesus declaring his own unique authority over against the traditional positions of Judaism. The opening section expresses this in succinct philosophical fashion (John 1:1-18), but the stories that follow unpack its meaning in down-to-earth terms. "The Jews" (especially Pharisees) are depicted as Jesus' opponents par excellence, much as they were in the writer's own day. The specific occasions on which Jesus crossed swords with the religious experts may not be identical with the synoptic stories, but the basic underlying issues were the same: Jesus' challenging of traditional spirituality, and his implicit claim (made more openly in John) that he himself embodied a new

Sixth-century mosaic of loaves and fishes in the Byzantine Church at Tabgha.

understanding of God's will. The ferocity of the opposition Jesus eventually encountered in Jerusalem is much easier to understand if these were themes that he had debated at some length with the religious leaders there long before that final week of his life.

Jesus . Their only previous experience of religion was to be put down by it. They were routinely disadvantaged and abused by those in positions of power – but Jesus turned the tables by treating them as people of value to God, and to their fellow human beings. Others would find a place for them in the system if they came grovelling and broken, confessing their sins and seeking forgiveness (and they sometimes did: the famous Rabbi Aqiba began life as one of the "people of the land"). But Jesus actively went out to mix with such people, to share their oppression – and in the process to open them up to new understandings of God. They may have been the "wrong" sort of people, but they were the ones whom God would welcome. The short parable of the Pharisee and the tax gatherer says it all: "all who exalt themselves will be humbled, but all who humble themselves will be exalted" (Luke 18:14).

It was bad enough for Jesus to mix with unsuitable people. But from time to time he also challenged the establishment and its ways of doing things more directly. In one of the first stories in

MAJOR RELIGIOUS INFLUENCES

The backdrop to the New Testament is provided by three cultures: Greek, Roman and Jewish. Many religious ideas and ideologies existed, often in conflict with each other.

■ Greek culture
The Roman empire was built upon Greek culture. Greek philosophy, learning and art was everywhere.

■ The Roman Empire
Roman rule dominated in every quarter: Roman taxes were levied from all subject states, the Roman "peace" was ensured by a strong and efficient military regime.

As well as traditional Greek and Roman religions, there were many religious sects propounding the way to salvation through a "secret" knowledge. These "Gnostics" believed in a pure, holy spirit world at odds with an evil, corrupt physical world. Some New Testament letters dealt severely with Gnostic belief.

Various "mystery" religions were also prevalent in the Roman empire, some arising from ancient Greek culture and some from the east. By nature secret societies, they were based on the cycles of the seasons, involving fertility rites and occult practices.

■ Judaism
Jewish religion is built on rigorous personal standards of morality, based on the Jewish scriptures. The Jewish scriptures were available in the Greek language and many Greeks and Romans were drawn to the Jewish faith and became "proselytes".

The Pharisees were the educators of the people and ensured the Jewish Law was applied to daily life.

The Sadducees came from the Jewish aristocracy, and controlled the position of high priest. They were concerned with preserving the priesthood and the place of the temple in Jewish life.

the gospel of John, Jesus went to the temple in Jerusalem, took a whip, and drove the merchants and bankers out (John 2:13-21). They had a right to be there, of course, though it was probably a recent concession granted to them not long before by the high priest Caiaphas as a means of undermining other markets set up outside the temple walls on the Mount of Olives. The purpose of this trade was simple. Most temple worship involved offering sacrifices, which meant that urban worshippers needed to buy animals when they got there. And since anything related to Rome was banned from the temple precincts – including its money – they needed to obtain the ritually approved currency before making a purchase. Both the merchants selling animals and the money-changers were therefore providing a useful service. But Jesus chased them out. The other gospels describe him doing this towards the end of his ministry. John places it at the beginning because it highlights so clearly the nature of the conflict between Jesus and the establishment: Jesus was determined to challenge a form of religiosity that would turn faith into a commodity to be bought, sold and controlled by self-opinionated experts. Jesus was convinced that anyone, no matter how ordinary, could have direct access to God. That meant people must come before procedures, regardless of how hallowed and venerable they might be. Even when a woman was caught in the very act of committing adultery, Jesus refused to condemn her, at the same time challenging her accusers with the words "Whichever one of you has committed no sin may throw the first stone at her" (John 8:1-11). For people at the bottom of the pile, valued by religious types at much less than birds and animals offered in sacrifice, it was good news indeed to be told that "you are worth much more than many sparrows" (Matthew 10:31).

THEOLOGY

The same conflict between people and structures underpins many of the conflict stories of the gospels. Conflict over the sabbath surfaces within the first two or three pages of Mark's gospel, and is never far from the centre of the action thereafter. Jesus was roundly condemned by religious leaders when he insisted on healing people on the sabbath, or allowed his disciples to pick

ears of grain as they walked through a cornfield (Mark 2:23-8, 3:1-6).

Family at work picking olives in Samaria.

This was more than an argument about social convention. Observance of the sabbath as a day of rest was enshrined in the Ten Commandments, which in turn claimed it went back to creation itself. According to the Old Testament, the people were to rest on the seventh day because "I the Lord made the earth, the sky, the sea, and everything in them, but on the seventh day I rested" (Exodus 20:11) . In Jesus' day, defining the sabbath was a major preoccupation of some religious experts. What does it mean to rest? Or, for that matter, for it to be the sabbath? For since in the Jewish reckoning, a day ran not from midnight to midnight, but from sunset to sunset, who could tell precisely when any given sabbath would begin and end? This last debate led to all sorts of bizarre arrangements, to ensure that people were not caught out still at work if the sun went down unexpectedly. For example, tailors were forbidden from going out carrying a needle in the afternoon before the sabbath started, in case they were caught out carrying the tools of their trade when sunset came – though they, like everyone else, could travel the permitted distance of 2000 cubits ("a sabbath day's journey"). Even that was less clear-cut than it might seem, and legal experts had worked out ways of going further without actually breaking the law. This was done by designating a point 2000 cubits from one's normal residence as "home" for the sabbath day, maybe by planting some food there in advance. Since a "sabbath day's journey" was reckoned to begin from "home", that gave a legal entitlement to travel at least 4000 cubits, if not more!

The same kind of perverse ingenuity was often applied to other laws as well, so that for those in the know it was possible to break the law, while still theoretically keeping it. In the light of practices like this, Jesus had good reason to ask why it was considered wrong to heal someone on the sabbath (Mark 3:4). What was supposed to be a day of rest had all too often become an excuse for religious fanatics to use the system to their own advantage, while finding fault with other people whose understanding of it differed from

Cloth for sale in the busy market at Beersheba.

JESUS' TEACHING ABOUT HIMSELF

As religions go, Judaism was amazingly flexible. As long as a person continued to observe the Law, there was room for plenty of diversity on other matters. Pharisees were quite different from Sadducees – but neither group accused the other of not being proper Jews! There was a range of permissible views on subjects. Even on something like the Messiah, there were several ideas. The most widely held expectation was certainly that the Messiah would be an ideal king descended from David. But in the Maccabean period the *Testament of the Twelve Patriarchs* provides evidence for belief in a Messiah from the priestly tribe of Levi (to which the Maccabees belonged). The Dead Sea

Scrolls also contain various ideas: a priestly Messiah and the (lay) Messiah of Israel; a "prophet" like Moses (mentioned in Deuteronomy 18:18-19), who is also identified with "the star" out of Jacob (Numbers 24:15-17); and the Davidic Messiah. The shadowy figure of Melchizedek also features there as a deliverer, though he is not actually called Messiah.

If Jesus had been merely a reformer within the Jewish tradition, then it is hard to account for the opposition he provoked. Yet there can be no denying the extreme antagonism felt towards him, certainly by the establishment, and perhaps more widely. Even in those violent days, people were not crucified for nothing. So what was it about Jesus that created such division of opinion? At one stage his family were convinced that he was mad (Mark 3:20-21). Others saw him as demon possessed (Mark 3:22-30) – a claim that was later repeated in the Talmud (*Sanhedrin* 43a). And ultimately, Pilate condemned him to death as "king of the Jews" (Mark 15:26). All the evidence shows that people believed Jesus was making pretensions to be far more important than he really was, centred on some kind of claim to have special – perhaps even unique – access to the will of God.

That is about as far as we can safely go. For as soon as we begin to ask specific questions about just exactly who and what Jesus thought he was, we are faced with a whole series of enigmas. Christians later in the New Testament period affirmed

without hesitation that Jesus was the Messiah. They even took the Greek term for Messiah ("Christ") and turned it into a kind of surname for Jesus. But can we categorically say that Jesus actually claimed to be the Messiah? What we can say is that many of Jesus' activities could easily be construed as a claim to messiahship. Things like the feeding of the five thousand, the repeated claim to be able to forgive sins, the casting out of demons, and the assertion that the Kingdom of God was present in his actions. But then when other people address Jesus as Messiah, he often instructs them to keep silent and not to let their beliefs be widely known.

The same is true of another favourite term of the early church, "son of God". The gospels have only a handful of examples of such language – and even then, its precise meaning is not absolutely clear, though it does suggest a special relationship to God (Mark 1:11, 9:7), as also does Jesus' boldness in addressing God as "Father" in prayer (Matthew 11:27, Mark 14:36).

There are two significant points where Mark uses the terminology of Messiah and Son of God. The first is in the story of Peter's confession at Caesarea Philippi. "Who do people say that I am?" asks Jesus – and Peter replies, "You are the Messiah" (Mark 8:27-30). This is followed by advice not to speak publicly about it, and then immediately Jesus goes on to talk about a figure he calls "the Son of Man". Much later, when Jesus stands on trial before the high priest, he is asked whether he is the Messiah – and here also he replies in terms of "the Son of Man" (Mark

14:61-62). Mark obviously understood these titles to be related in some way, and it is tempting to suppose that Jesus deliberately avoided use of the word "Messiah" precisely because he wanted to distance himself from most of the popular understandings of who the Messiah would be and what kind of things he would do. By calling himself "Son of Man", was he perhaps using a term that was, at best, ambiguous – but for that reason, one he could infuse with his own distinctive understanding of his role?

To answer that question, we must ask another: who was the Son of Man? A simple enough question, to which there is no simple answer. More uncertainty surrounds this issue than just about anything else in the entire New Testament. It is not even clear what – if anything – the term might have meant in first century Judaism. The phrase itself is an awkward one, grammatically speaking. The actual words would make no sense at all in Greek, which suggests its background is to be found in either Aramaic or Hebrew usage. But there is very little evidence here to point us in the right direction. The few texts with a phrase like this seem to use it to mean something like "humankind" or "people in general". In the Old Testament, it appears in two contexts. In some places it means "humankind" (e.g. Numbers 23:19, Psalm 8:4), and can be applied to individuals as a way of emphasising the difference between them and the mighty power of God (Ezekiel 2:1, Daniel 8:17). But in Daniel 7:13-14, it designates a figure of great spiritual power who, at the end of

time, receives from "the Ancient of Days ... an everlasting dominion, which shall not pass away, and a kingdom ... that shall not be destroyed." A similar concept is found in the *Similitudes of Enoch*, a Jewish writing that could be roughly contemporaneous with the New Testament.

There has been endless expert analysis of all this, ranging over a whole variety of questions. Did Jesus use the term at all? And if so, was it the equivalent of the English word "one", used as a way of referring to himself – or was he claiming to be the Son of Man who would come in the future, or the Son of Man who would suffer and die here and now? If he used the term, what did he want people to take out of it? The debates still continue, and about the only certain conclusion is that the term "Son of Man" had no simple and immediately obvious meaning to the people of first century Palestine. In this respect it was quite different from other words such as Messiah or Son of God. Perhaps this was why it appealed to Jesus. It was, at best, an ambiguous term, which meant Jesus could make it mean what he wanted. But at the same time, for those well acquainted with the scriptures, the way it was used there could provide clues to some of the things Jesus wanted to claim for himself. For he did want to claim both that he was an ordinary human being (that was why people so easily related to him); and also that he was specially sent from God (and that was why they could trust him).

Traditional ideas of the Messiah certainly did not sit comfortably with Jesus' message. His view that brute force is not God's way would have

little to commend it to those with a militaristic mind-set. Nor would his conviction that love is more important than power. And what oriental king could ever agree that people are more valuable than systems, structures and programmes? Jesus broke away from all that, demonstrating in his own lifestyle that a true leader leads from alongside, not from above, and reminding his disciples at every opportunity that faithfulness to God's will often leads to suffering. Jesus exemplified all this in his own dealings with other people, and in the process challenged their perceptions of the very nature of God. The God whom Jesus related to, and to whom he introduced his disciples, was not a tyrant remote from the concerns of ordinary people, but a loving parent to whom women and men could relate as easily as they did to their own mother or father. That alone was such a radical claim, it was a foregone conclusion that it would provoke outspoken opposition.

their own. People were being strangled by their own rules. But Jesus reversed this, insisting that in God's way of looking at things people come first, and institutions second: "The sabbath was made for humankind, and not humankind for the sabbath" (Mark 2:27).

Nor was this an isolated example. The same thing happened with rituals for washing and eating food. Centuries before, the high priest had been required to wash his hands before entering the tent of worship (Exodus 30:19, 40:13). But by the time of Jesus, many devout people had adopted this practice as part of everyday life, and they regularly washed their hands first thing in the morning, and before meals. Not for reasons of hygiene, as we may do today, but for religious purposes, to ensure their ritual purity. None of this was required by the Old Testament laws, which only gave more scope for later rule-makers, who had even developed regulations prescribing exactly which bits of the hands should be washed to preserve ritual purity. When you blend all this with the already complex dietary rules of the Old Testament itself, then even a simple thing like eating food had the potential to spark off acrimonious religious debate. When Jesus was challenged about his own failure to keep all these regulations, he did not enter into discussion on the issue. He simply stated (quoting Isaiah) that so far as he was concerned, rules of this sort were unnecessary additions to the scripture: "you abandon the commandment of God and hold to human tradition" (Mark 7:8). As if to reinforce his indifference to such things, he went on to talk about the things that really make a person unclean – like "greed, deceit, indecency, jealousy, slander, pride and folly." (Mark 7:22).

Yet even some of those practices could be justified by reference to religious and legal tradition! If you knew how to do it, it was not difficult to exploit the system for personal advantage – for example, by consecrating money to God as a way to avoid sharing it with other members of the family (Mark 7:9-13). A person could appear exceedingly righteous by observing various minor rules and regulations, while side-stepping the central challenge of the Old Testament to "Love the Lord your God ... and love your neighbour as you love yourself" (Mark 12: 29-31).

Jesus was obviously well acquainted with such sanctimonious hypocrisy, which raises an interesting question. If all this was not official Pharisaic belief, then how did Jesus know so much about the devious behaviour of certain sections of the religious establishment? Did he have some personal experience of it? Was he so violently opposed to the Pharisees because members of his own family in fact belonged to that group? Certainly, most Pharisees would be in the same social class as a tradesman like Joseph – and when Jesus' brother, James, later became a Christian, he not only displayed highly conservative inclinations, but also had connections with "believers who belonged to the party of the Pharisees" (Acts 15:5). Could this also explain the ferocity of the establishment's opposition to Jesus, as well as putting in a new perspective the deep hostility of his own family (including even Mary, at least until the time of his death)?

Jesus undoubtedly challenged some fairly central aspects of Jewish practice in his day. For example, the Old Testament certainly did lay down the death penalty for adultery; it certainly

SOME NAMES AND TITLES OF JESUS

■ **Jesus**
A Greek version of a common Hebrew name: Joshua, or Jeshua, meaning "Yahweh (The Lord) is my help".

■ **Lord**
The Greek version of the Old Testament used the word "Lord" (*kurios*) as God's personal name. The early Christians had no hesitation in applying it to Jesus.

■ **Son of man**
Jesus' chosen name, echoing a vision of the prophet Daniel. Jesus took this unusual title and applied it to stress both his human and divine natures.

■ **Messiah**
Meaning "the anointed one". The Greek equivalent is "Christ", and became part of Jesus' name – Jesus Christ. Anointing was a sign that God had chosen and prepared a person for his own special purpose. Many in Jesus' day looked for the coming of the "Messiah". Interestingly, Jesus did not emphasize this aspect of his ministry.

■ **Son of God**
This title is used especially in John's gospel to emphasise Jesus' unique relationship to God. Jesus himself addressed God as "Father", and encouraged the disciples to do the same.

■ **Son of David**
Born through the line of King David, and born in Bethlehem, David's city, Jesus fulfilled Old Testament prophecies concerning the coming of the Messiah. Despite this, the Jews refused to recognise Jesus as such.

■ **I am**
Jesus used this phrase of himself several times in the gospels, especially in John. It recalls God's revelation to Moses as "I am who I am" (in Hebrew "Yahweh", and is another way of indicating Jesus' close relationship with God.

■ **The lamb**
The blood of the Passover sacrifice was the means of salvation for the people of Israel, and Isaiah describes God's servant as "like a lamb that is taken to be slaughtered". Many disciples saw the parallel with Jesus.

encouraged keeping the sabbath day; and it insisted that food should be eaten only within certain prescribed limits. When Jesus apparently set aside all of these, and more, it was natural that those who were trying to remain faithful to the old traditions saw him simply as a heretic.

But his theological challenge involved more than merely pragmatic considerations about food, the calendar and personal morality. Early in his ministry he returned to Nazareth, to share his teaching with those who knew him best. When he stood up to address the congregation in the synagogue, his listeners expected him to read and expound the scripture – something he had probably done there on many previous occasions. But this time, he went much further. Having read a passage that was widely believed to relate to the coming messianic age (Isaiah 61:1-2), he had the affrontery to declare "This passage of scripture has come true today, as you heard it being read" (Luke 4:21). Though no claims to messiahship were made explicitly, this statement quite obviously

Bedouin woman preparing unleavened bread in the traditional way.

MIRACLES

In his sermon at the synagogue in Nazareth, Jesus referred to a passage from Isaiah which celebrated the fact that the messianic age would bring "good news to the poor ... liberty to the captives and recovery of sight to the blind" (Luke 4:18). Words were an important part of Jesus' message. But they were not the only element, and the deeds we call miracles also played a significant role both in his popular appeal and the opposition that he encountered. It was not so much that people regarded the miracles as a hoax. Rather, they were not considered indicators that God was at work in his life. There were prophets – and false prophets. And Jesus was one of the latter. In Mark 3, certain scribes offered the opinion that he was inspired by "the chief of the demons", which is why he found it so easy to drive them out (3:22), and this was a popular Jewish viewpoint. Josephus passes no judgment on the origin of Jesus' powers, but he does confirm that he had them, describing him as "a doer of wonderful deeds, and a teacher of those who receive the truth gladly" (*Antiquities of the Jews* 18.63-4).

For modern readers, this is not the most obvious starting point. Influenced by the scientific rationalism that has permeated western culture for the last two or three hundred years, we would be more inclined to put the miracle stories down to the ignorance and superstition of ancient people. As the twentieth century has progressed, this opinion has become much less credible than it once seemed. On the one hand, the chauvinistic attitude that presumed all ancient people were either fools or frauds is now seen for what it is: a form of personal arrogance and downright snobbery. There is plenty of evidence to show that ancient people were no more gullible or naive than their modern counterparts. In addition, the more science has discovered, the more mysteries there are about many things, illness and its cures being prominent among them. And as knowledge of cultures outside the west has increased, it has become increasingly obvious that it is rationalism, with its insistence on "logical" explanations of cause-and-effect that is the aberration, not the belief in a spiritual world that is beyond what we normally see and handle. When the majority of the world's people have no hesitation in accepting the reality of such things, it is only an outmoded and defensive form of intellectual and cultural imperialism that will question it. If anyone doubts that, they need only look around at the way the New Age movement has put the miraculous and supernatural very firmly back on to the western agenda.

In point of fact, Jesus' work as a healer was not that distinctive at the time. Jesus himself referred – apparently with approval – to other people who were casting out demons (Matthew 12:27), and he expected his own disciples to exercise the same sort of ministry (Mark 6:7, 13). Both Jewish and Roman literature of the day contain stories of healing miracles of various sorts. Of course, in understanding what was going on, we cannot return to a first century mentality, and from our perspective it is inevitable that we will want to ask what was actually happening. When is a miracle a miracle? Someone in a primitive tribe might see a modern invention like television and regard it as a miracle. Another person will know how it works, and describe it differently. A mother with a long history of miscarriages and stillbirths has a healthy baby, and regards it as a miracle. Someone else can point to the statistics, and say it was bound to happen sooner or later. People can look at the same event and, depending on their perspective, make rather different assessments of what has taken place. For example, we now know that there is a close link between mind and body, and even quite striking physical ailments like cancer can, on occasion, have psychological roots. It would be surprising if some of the illnesses cured by Jesus were not psychosomatic, as we would say nowadays – and some gospel stories seem to hint as much. For instance, the account of how Jesus healed a woman with a haemorrhage merely by her touching his clothes (Mark 5:25-34) – or when he cured a blind man by mixing clay and placing it on his eyes (John 9:1-11).

The distinctive thing about Jesus' miracles is not so much what he did, but when he did it – and to whom. It is striking that the kind of people Jesus healed – the deaf, dumb, and lame – do not feature at all in contemporary stories of Jewish healers. But these were the very things singled out as signs of the coming kingdom in an Old Testament passage that was widely regarded as messianic (Isaiah

A general view of the town of Nazareth.

then it had to take seriously the problem of disease. There was, therefore, a very strong theological underpinning to Jesus' miracles, and it was this to which his opponents took exception. For when we look closely at the miracles, we uncover the same underlying themes as we have noticed in his lifestyle. God is presented as a loving parent, who cares for all people without exception. Just as Jesus taught in words and attitudes that God loves all kinds of people, so his miracles often involved the outcasts of society – showing that his declaration of God's care and concern was not just talk, but demanded action (Matthew 8:1-4, Luke 17:11-19, Mark 5:21-43). Healing and forgiveness also went hand in hand (Mark 2:1-12), while faith was called for on the part of those who would be healed (Mark 5:32-4, 9:14-29), and at least one story implies that the absence of faith could be a hindrance to the work of healing (Mark 6:5-6). Need we look further to see why the miracles would provoke opposition?

35:5-6). The coincidence would not be lost on those who were suspicious of Jesus' intentions. Nor would it escape their attention that the circumstances in which he cured people often infringed Jewish laws. Not only did Jesus heal people on the sabbath, but he also healed those who were non-people so far as Jewish ritual purity was concerned. People of the wrong racial origins (such as the Gentile woman in Mark 7:24-30). People who lived in the wrong kind of places (like the man in the pagan graveyard in Mark 5:1-20). And people who by any definition were ritually impure (such as the woman with a permanent menstrual flow, Mark 5:25-34).

How could anyone of goodwill possibly be opposed to the healing of those who were suffering? That was the commonsense question asked by Jesus when he cured a man with a paralysed hand in the synagogue (Mark 3:4). On that level, any opposition would seem particularly perverse. But Jesus did not primarily heal people because he was sorry for them. He saw disadvantage of any kind as a sign that the power of Satan was at work – and so, for example he was "filled with anger" at the sight of a man disfigured by leprosy (Mark 1:40-45). He did not of course identify suffering with personal sin, or suggest that the sufferer was somehow responsible for the misfortune. Quite the reverse: when the Pharisees proposed that to him, he categorically denied it (John 9:1-5).

But if God's Kingdom was to displace "the kingdom of this world", implied that Jesus was special, and had some distinctive understanding of the will of God.

The same kind of claim is taken for granted in other stories. For example, when Jesus offered to forgive sins, he was met with the criticism that "This is blasphemy! God is the only one who can forgive sins" (Mark 2:7). The casting out of demons laid him open to the same charge (Mark 3:20-30). In John's gospel, Jesus makes openly messianic claims from the outset, and in the various "I am" sayings seems to be taking for himself the

SOME OF JESUS' MIRACLES IN THE GOSPELS

	Matthew	Mark	Luke	John
Peter's mother-in-law healed	8:14-5	1:29-31	4:38-9	
Water into wine				2:1-11
Miraculous catch of fish			5:1-11	
Centurion's servant healed	8:5-13		7:1-10	
The storm calmed	8:22-37	4:35-41	8:22-5	
Demoniac healed	8:28-34	5:1-20	8:26-39	
Paralysed man healed	9:1-8	2:1-12	5:17-26	
Jairus' daughter healed	9:18-26	5:21-43	8:40-56	
Widow's son raised from death			7:11-17	
Feeding 5000	14:13-21	6:30-44	9:10-7	6:1-14
Walking on water	14:22-33	6:45-52		
Feeding 4000	15:32-9	8:1-10		
Blind man healed at Bethsaida		8:22-26		
Man blind from birth healed				9:1-12
Epileptic boy healed	17:14-21	9:14-29	9:37-43	
Ten lepers healed			17:11-9	
Lazarus raised from death				11:1-44
Blind Bartimaeus healed	20:29-34	10:46-52	18:35-43	

traditional authority of God in the Old Testament. The synoptic gospels more usually depict him trying to hush up any idea that he could be the Messiah, though even there he eventually gives a straight answer to the high priest's question, "Are you the Messiah, the Son of the Blessed God?", replying simply "I am" – though then going on to define what that meant in terms of his own preferred title for himself, the Son of Man (Mark 14:61-2).

BELIEF AND UNBELIEF

The gospels contrast the growing unbelief and opposition of the religious establishment with the developing commitment of the disciples. The episode at Caesarea Philippi, when Peter made his faith confession that "You are the Messiah", is in many ways the centre point of the whole story (Mark 8:27-30). Though the term is never used, Peter is presented as a typical member of that undervalued group, "the people of the land". *Looking from Mount Hermon* When he later appeared before a Jewish court *toward Caesarea Philippi* accused with John of being one of Jesus' *(modern Banyas).* accomplices, they were described as "uneducated

and ordinary men" – people who could not normally be expected to have much understanding of religious affairs (Acts 4:13). The way his faith in Jesus gradually developed is also in strong contrast to religious experts who know all the answers. When he declared Jesus to be the Messiah, Peter really had no idea what it might mean, and immediately afterwards he found himself being dismissed by Jesus as "Satan" – "for you are setting your mind not on divine things but on human things" (Mark 8:33). Yet Peter had that genuine integrity that Jesus found so strikingly missing in many professional theologians. What he lacked in conventional knowledge he more than made up for in enthusiasm and spiritual openness. He was ready to accept when he was wrong, and to learn from his mistakes. He knew he had not arrived, spiritually speaking, but he was the more genuine a person for that. An honest seeker after truth, who was always prepared to give what he knew of himself to what he understood of God.

The contrast between the growing faith of the disciples and the increasingly blind opposition of others continues through the rest of the story. As Jesus questions and challenges the accepted opinions, he both attracts and repels, until the opposition becomes overwhelming and the story eventually moves towards a showdown in Jerusalem. But before we get to that, we must pause to take an even closer look at some of Jesus' teachings.

JESUS AND
HIS MESSAGE

JESUS THE TEACHER

I N THE ancient world, teachers were always given a place of
special importance. Roman and Greek culture had a long
tradition of philosophical schools, going back to the time
(centuries before Jesus) when eager students had sat at the feet of
intellectual giants such as Plato or Socrates, hoping to discover
the meaning of life. Though times changed, when the earliest
disciples of Jesus took their message out into the great cities of
the Roman empire, there was still no shortage of people who
were happy to spend time listening to a good teacher.

Jesus never set foot in ancient Greece or Rome, but he too was
brought up in a culture that placed great value on the spoken
word. There were books, of course – predominant among which
was the Hebrew Bible (Old Testament), which was written down
long before Jesus' day and was the subject of intense study by
those with a special vocation for such things. The professional
students of the Law – scribes and others – made it their lifetime's
work to become familiar with the ancient scriptures, and then to
share their learning with the rest of the people. These books were
written in Hebrew, a language which not everyone could read, and
it was a special privilege for a boy (never a girl) to be taught
Hebrew in the local synagogue school, and then eventually to gain
direct access to the ancient traditions of his people. But most
ordinary people had to learn by listening, not by reading.
Listening to the scriptures as they were read in worship each
sabbath. Listening, too, as they were translated into Aramaic, the
language most people spoke (a process that eventually led to the
production of written Aramaic versions, the Targums). And
listening to the exhortations of the rabbis, as they sought to
explain what the requirements of the Law meant in terms of
everyday life and behaviour.

Everyone recognised Jesus as a religious teacher. Not only his
disciples, but his opponents, and people in general – they all
referred to him as a rabbi (the Aramaic word for teacher,
probably just used as a term of respect in Jesus' day). He had the
opportunity to teach in the local synagogues, and in the temple at
Jerusalem, as well as speaking in fields and market places

*Jerusalem. Sephardic Jew
at study.*

wherever he went. People came to ask Jesus for his opinion on points of law and religion, in much the same way as they did with the other rabbis. In response to questions, he dealt with matters such as divorce and marriage (Mark 10:1-12), adultery (John 7:53-8:11), family quarrels (Luke 12:13-15), and paying taxes (Mark 12:13-17), as well as more theological matters such as the commandments (Mark 12:28-34), or belief in resurrection (Mark 12:18-27), or the reasons for undeserved suffering (John 9:2-3).

Jewish people had a long tradition of such teaching. The Hebrew Bible itself was no doubt handed on by word of mouth for many generations before it was eventually written down. Much of its content consists of the written text of teaching that was originally delivered orally. The prophets of the Old Testament were speakers, not writers. And the pithy sayings contained in a book like Proverbs were obviously the sort of everyday wisdom that would be passed on verbally from one generation to another. The book of Psalms consists of hymns that were meant to be sung in worship, while many people believe the book of Job was a play that would be performed on stage.

The spoken word was always held in high esteem. Even into the second century, we find Papias, leader of the Christian community at Hierapolis in Asia Minor, writing that "what was to be got from books was not so profitable to me as what came from the living and abiding voice" (reported in Eusebius, *Ecclesiastical History* iii.39). Perhaps this explains why it took the early Christians so long to get around to writing the gospels. They actually preferred to listen rather than to read!

THE KINGDOM OF GOD

The Kingdom of God is the major theme of Jesus' teaching in the gospels of Matthew, Mark and Luke. Matthew uses the term "kingdom of heaven" to mean the same thing – no doubt in deference to the sensitivities of his original readers, who were from a strict Jewish background and may have been offended by the bold and continual use of the name of God. Mark and Luke had no such inhibitions, for their readers were Gentiles, living in cities of the Roman empire far removed from Judea and its narrow religious concerns.

From the very beginning of Israelite history, God had always been regarded as "king" of the people. The Old Testament declares that the whole world belongs to God, because God made it – and Israel as a nation belongs to God because God rescued their ancestors from slavery in Egypt and gave them a new land. When they wanted to appoint Saul as their own king a century or two later, some people opposed the move on the grounds that God was the only true king the nation could ever have. Subsequently, when David became king in Jerusalem, the two ideas were brought together. David and his successors were the rightful rulers of the nation – because God had chosen them. Their duty was to do God's will, so that the kingdom would reflect the values and standards of God's law.

But things were never that simple. As one king succeeded another, it was painfully obvious that many of them were only interested in power and self-fulfilment, and the earlier ideals gradually disappeared. They certainly disappeared as practical politics. But they never quite vanished altogether. For they were transformed into a hope for the future, that – somewhere, sometime – God would step in to put things right and establish a kingdom of justice and right. The prophet Zechariah was only one of many who fervently looked for that time to come – a day on which "the Lord will become king over all the earth" (Zechariah 14:9). By the time of Jesus, there was a widespread expectation that the arrival of the Messiah would herald the coming of this kingdom.

Jesus' message about the Kingdom of God has many sides to it. In an earlier generation, scholars spent much time trying to decide whether Jesus was looking for some future cataclysmic happening that would usher in the Kingdom in some tangible form, and signal the end of the world – or whether he was talking instead of some internal spiritual disposition on the part of his followers. But these two things are not contradictory: they are two sides of the same coin.

In some passages, Jesus undoubtedly does describe the Kingdom in ways that seem to imply the final winding-up of all history. He talks of the last judgment, of the Son of Man coming with the clouds

PARABLES AND PROVERBS

Jesus' teaching was characterised by memorable stories and sayings. To hold people's attention, a teacher must be interesting, and Jesus was an expert at this. His style did not centre on abstract theological truths, but on the living experience of his hearers. As a creative thinker himself, he recognised the power of story telling. Stories seize the imagination. But they also create an open space in which people can reflect, and draw their own conclusions. No two people take exactly the same lesson out of a story. Jesus obviously had this art of communication highly developed. People immediately recognised that he was different from other teachers (Mark 1:22). Other rabbis often insisted their disciples should learn their teachings off by heart. But Jesus

of heaven, and of how his followers will "inherit the kingdom" (Matthew 25:34) – where they will be joined by people who will "come from east and west, and from north and south, and sit at table in the kingdom of God" (Luke 13:29). At his last meal with his disciples, he told them "From now on I shall not drink of the fruit of the vine until the kingdom of God comes" (Luke 22:18). And, in less dramatic ways, he speaks of the Kingdom growing like yeast or mustard seeds until it begins to challenge and change social structures (Matthew 13:31-3).

At the same time, Jesus also told one questioner that "The kingdom of God does not come in such a way as to be seen ... the kingdom of God is within you" (Luke 17:20-21). Other passages also seem to imply that people are judged not in some dim and distant future, but by their responses to his teaching (Mark 3:28-30) – something that is made quite explicit in the statement in John's gospel that "Those who believe in him are not condemned;

but those who do not believe are condemned already, because they have not believed in the name of the only Son of God. And this is the judgment, that the light has come into the world, and people loved darkness rather than light, because their deeds were evil" (John 3:18-19).

This paradoxical tension between what is future and what is present would be quite familiar to Jewish people. At the time of Jesus, many of the rabbis were teaching that God's kingship over Israel was already in operation, even while the Romans were in control – and that it operated through the Torah, or Law. They sometimes referred to people "taking upon themselves the Kingdom of God", by which they meant accepting and keeping God's law as the sign of God's rule over them. He did not demand obedience to the Law, but Jesus saw things in fundamentally the same way. He could encourage his disciples to pray, "your kingdom come" (Matthew 5:10), while also assuring them that "there are some standing here who will not taste

death until they see that the kingdom of God has come with power" (Mark 9:1), and telling John the Baptist that the kingdom had already arrived in his own person (Luke 7:18-23). The Kingdom arrived in essence in the person of Jesus himself. Its power was expressed through the events of his death and resurrection and the coming of the Holy Spirit to his disciples. And its full effect will be seen at that point in time when his followers, working like salt, light, and yeast have taken his message to all corners of the earth. Meanwhile, wherever women and men accept and promote the values of the Kingdom, there it is already established in embryonic form.

gave people freedom to think for themselves, and encouraged them to work out what God was saying to them personally in their own particular circumstances of life.

The extended stories that Jesus told are called parables. But so are much shorter sayings. A popular proverb such as "Physician, heal yourself" is called a "parable" (Luke 4:23), as also is the saying, "Can a blind person guide a blind person?" (Luke 6:39). While the same terminology is applied to the more or less factual statement (perhaps originally some kind of riddle?) that "there is nothing outside a person that by going in can defile, but the things that come out are what defile" (Mark 7:15-16). There are also many other places where Jesus uses words to conjure up a vivid mental image that will help to communicate his message. In the Sermon on the Mount (Matthew 5-7) he talks of salt, light, a city, birds, and flowers, while in John's gospel he describes himself as "the good shepherd" (10:1-18), "the true vine" (15:1-11), bread (6:35), or life-giving water (7:37-9), and talks of the disciples being called to reap a harvest (4:31-8). By using this kind of graphic language, Jesus ensured that his

Bedouin encampment and sheep teachings would be remembered without
in the hill country of Samaria. difficulty. Instead of speaking in abstractions, as

modern western religious teachers tend to do, Jesus always spoke of concrete situations and people. Jesus did not say, "Materialism can be a hindrance to spiritual growth", but "No-one can be a slave of two masters ... You cannot serve God and money" (Matthew 6:24). That kind of expression is not easily forgotten, for it immediately relates to people's everyday experience of life.

Jesus frequently used extreme exaggeration to make his point. For example, he said that it is better to pull one's eye out rather than to commit adultery, or better to cut one's hand off rather than displease God (Matthew 5:29). He was obviously not meaning to suggest that disciples should do either of these things (they certainly never thought so, anyway, for there is no evidence that they believed it was spiritual to mutilate themselves!). But he used this extravagant language to impress on his hearers the seriousness of his message.

Jesus also used poetry, though people with no knowledge of Aramaic will not usually recognise it as such. English poetry depends for its effect on rhyme or stress, but Hebrew and

JESUS MEETS THE PEOPLE

Wherever we look in the gospels, Jesus is presented as a person who was impatient with the theological hair-splitting of religious experts. It was not his style to engage in abstract debates, nor was he particularly interested in intellectual knowledge for its own sake. His whole life was dedicated to people, and his message was concerned with their needs.

The gospels paint many vivid thumb-nail sketches of Jesus at work among people. Dancing with them, drinking with them, in casual conversations in fields and market places – but always with a view to bringing healing and renewal into their lives, as he pointed them to God and the Kingdom. The fact that Jesus

engaged in so many "ordinary" things at once marked him out as different. But that was not his only attraction for people who were normally considered well beyond the pale of respectable religion. We could choose any one of a large number of stories to illustrate why Jesus was so captivating. But there is one in particular that combines so many themes it provides a more comprehensive model than most. This is the story in John 4, of how Jesus met a woman by a well, in the most unpromising circumstances, how he invited her to discipleship, and how she not only accepted the challenge but went off to share it with others from her village.

One of the most surprising

features of this whole encounter is just the simple fact that Jesus was there at all. Everything was out of joint in terms of the conventions of his day. For a start, women were not typically considered capable of receiving religious teaching from a rabbi. Even a relatively enlightened teacher like the second century rabbi Jose ben Johanan could freely open his home to the homeless and destitute, but still advised: "Talk not with womankind ... He that talks much with womankind brings evil upon himself and neglects the study of the Law and at the last will inherit Gehenna" (*Aboth* 1.5). It was unusual enough that a religious teacher like Jesus should take a woman seriously. But this one was a Samaritan, a member of a group who were hated more than most by Jewish people.

Aramaic poetry operated with correspondences of thought (called parallelism). There were two major forms of poetry, depending on whether the correspondence was one of similarity or difference. "Do not give dogs what is holy; and do not throw your pearls before swine", said Jesus (Matthew 7:6) – an example of "synonymous parallelism" in which the second line repeats the thought of the first, but using different imagery. Then there was "antithetical parallelism", where the same idea was taught in each line, but using exactly opposite concepts, as when Jesus observed that "Every sound tree bears good fruit, but the bad tree bears bad fruit" (Matthew 7:17). Even the Lord's Prayer can be arranged in poetic stanzas, and was obviously couched in this way so that it would be easy to remember.

Outside Bethlehem. Drawing water from a well.

WHAT WAS JESUS' MESSAGE?

Towards the beginning of his gospel, Mark sums up Jesus' teaching in a single sentence: "The time is fulfilled, and the

There is some dispute as to who exactly the Samaritans of New Testament times were. They may have been the descendants of half-Jewish people who opposed the introduction of strict religious laws after the Jewish exiles returned to Jerusalem from Babylon back in the third and fourth centuries before Christ. More probably, they were a new sect that had emerged in the days just before the beginning of the Christian era. In any event, to be a Samaritan was bad news for devout Jews. Samaritans had their own customs – religious and civil – and their own place of worship. Their land was located between Galilee and Judea, and to get from one to the other rigorous law-keepers would have made a long detour east of the Jordan river, rather than risk contamination by travelling through

Samaria. But Jesus had no such inhibitions. He did not require that people should meet him on territory where only he felt safe, where he was in control and could determine the outcome. Jesus went out to where people actually were, and willingly made himself weak and vulnerable in order to communicate.

Just how vulnerable becomes obvious from the circumstances. The well was on a remote hillside. It was a hot day. Jesus was desperately thirsty – and only the woman had the means with which to get water! She was a woman with a lot of experience with men. As the story unfolds, we learn that she had been married five times, and was cohabiting with a sixth man. She had plenty of experience of abuse at the hands of men, and the last thing she wanted out in this remote spot

was to be exploited yet again. Jesus knew he was speaking with a doubly disadvantaged person. So where did he begin? Right from the start, Jesus got alongside her. First of all, he revealed that he had a need: he was desperately thirsty. More than that, it was a need that she could meet. And so he asked if she would share her water with him. He made himself vulnerable in a big way. But in so doing he also affirmed her as a person of value, and right away the woman recognised something unusual was happening. Instead of the lecture she might have expected, putting her down by complaining about all that was wrong with her, this was to be a two-way conversation. A rabbi who would actually listen – to a woman, and a Samaritan! Moreover, a rabbi who was prepared to ask questions – and

actually pay attention to another person's answers. Jesus was a great listener, and that was one of the secrets of his appeal to disadvantaged people: he had time to hear what they wanted to say.

Not only that, but Jesus was prepared to follow the woman's own agenda. He did not focus on communicating a set of abstract ideas, but on the questions the woman was actually asking. Jesus always addressed people at their point of need, and began where people were. When he met fishermen by the Sea of Galilee, he talked about fish. With a rich man, the subject was money. With this woman at the well, he began with the water. He followed an adaptive strategy. Jesus

was not primarily message-centred, but people-centred. Some modern Christians feel uncomfortable with the fact that Jesus' message was not expressed in the same terms for

everyone. It can come as a surprise to learn that only once did Jesus mention being "born again" (John 3:3), or require a person to "sell all you have" (Mark 10:21). Jesus knew

Jerusalem. Bedouin women with dried figs and fruit for sale.

kingdom of God has come near; repent, and believe in the good news" (Mark 1:14). The rest of the story of Jesus both explains and illustrates the meaning of this statement.

"The time is fulfilled", Jesus declared. His hearers would have little doubt which time Jesus was talking about. For centuries, their people had been looking for the arrival of the Messiah, who when he came would correct all that was out of joint in both national and personal life. Some, of course, were looking for little more than the restoration of a Jewish national identity, and the expulsion of the hated Romans from their land. But many others recognised deeper needs within themselves. The need for inner strength to come to terms with their own wounded spirits. The need for a new power to enable them to do what was right. The need for the broken fragments of their lives to be reconstructed with love and compassion, so they might yet become channels of new meaning and blessing to others. As the story of Jesus unfolds, it soon becomes obvious that these are the people for whom the time is most truly fulfilled. The marginalised, the oppressed, the

his message would only be taken seriously if it was relevant for each person and situation.

As it happens, the woman did not immediately express her deepest needs to Jesus. Perhaps she was still too threatened by her previous experiences to do so. But Jesus had some unusual insights. An earlier passage in John states that "he knew all people and needed no one to testify about anyone; for he himself knew what was in everyone" (2:24-5). Other gospels make similar claims. Luke frequently reports not only Jesus' openness to all sorts of outcasts of society (a Samaritan even makes it as one of the heroes of the parables in Luke 10:25-37), but also the fact that Jesus consciously relied on the special insights of the Holy Spirit to apply his message to the concerns of his hearers. This is what

happened here. Jesus had no prior knowledge of the woman's home circumstances, but when he revealed them to her in such detail, she knew for sure that he was "a prophet" – maybe even "the prophet" foretold by Moses.

Having moved the woman on in her understanding, Jesus was in a uniquely credible position from which to challenge her about discipleship. This was always Jesus' style. Though repentance and forgiveness were central to his understanding of God's Kingdom, he never put people down. Just as he had done with Peter by the shore of Galilee, so with this woman he never spoke of her sinfulness. She was already well aware of her own inadequacy, but precisely because Jesus gave her time and space to come to terms with it in her own

way, she was happy enough to go back to the village to share her experiences with her friends. For such a person – a woman (maybe even a prostitute) and a Samaritan – this was good news indeed. A religious teacher who lifted her up, left her feeling affirmed and valued, must be someone special in the purposes of God.

downcast and disheartened: all find a special place in the heart of Jesus. Tax gatherers, prostitutes, lepers, children, the demon-possessed, ordinary workers of all sorts. These are the people for whom the time has come. Their pain and suffering has been noticed. Their cry has been heard. Their lives can be changed. "The Kingdom of God has come near".

So what is this "Kingdom of God"? We can usefully begin by saying what it is not. The Kingdom of God is certainly not a place or a structure or an institution. Back in the fourth century, Augustine imagined that the Kingdom was just another name for the church. Nearer to our own times, European explorers often supposed that by imposing their own civilisation on people in other parts of the world, they too were somehow setting up God's Kingdom. But we can be quite sure that, whatever Jesus meant by it, the Kingdom of God was none of these things.

In some respects, the word "Kingdom" is an unfortunate translation of the original Aramaic words that Jesus would use. God's "Kingdom" is really God's sovereignty. People have a part in God's Kingdom when they accept God as sovereign in their lives, and seek to live in accordance with God's values and standards. God's Kingdom is a new quality of life — whether individual or social — which is available to those who are prepared to open themselves to the presence of God's Spirit. Indeed, in some passages "entering the Kingdom". is identified with "entering into life" (Mark 9:43-7, Matthew 25:34-46). When a rich man came to Jesus asking "what must I do to inherit eternal life", and was then unable to accept Jesus' advice to give his goods to the poor, Jesus observed, "How hard it will be for those who have wealth to enter the kingdom of God" (Mark 10:17-23). The enjoyment of life lived to the full is a constant theme of Jesus' teaching in John's gospel, where he declares without hesitation, "I came that they may have life, and have it abundantly" (John 10:10).

This explains how Jesus could say that "the Kingdom of God is within you ..." (Luke 17:20-21). He was clearly not suggesting that we are all somehow a part of God — for Jesus also insisted that a person needs to "enter" the Kingdom, and they enter it when they "receive the kingdom of God like a child" (Mark 10:15). Adults find it very hard to receive anything. We prefer to give, for we all like to be strong, and in control of things. But according to Jesus, if anyone makes it into God's Kingdom, it will not be by their possession of any special qualifications or personal insight, but through God's sheer love and goodness. People get into the Kingdom because God wants them in – and they get in when they are prepared to receive what God can give, without looking for ways of justifying themselves.

This is the theme of some of Jesus' most striking parables. The three stories in Luke 15 all make this point. There is the lost sheep, who is found because the shepherd cares and goes out in search of the wanderer. The lost coin, which comes to light as its owner diligently sweeps through her entire house. And the lost son, who finds himself living in poverty in a hostile environment, when he could be back home with his family. Even then, though he recognises that he needs to go home, he finds himself at the centre of a controversy. In this case, the son himself knows his own weakness, and is ready enough to accept his parent's generosity. Too ready, in the opinion of his brother, who like so many finds it hard to accept that anyone should get something for nothing.

Then there is the story of men looking for work. Following the regular custom of the day, they gathered in the market place first thing in the morning, to see who would hire them. A vineyard owner came along and gave a job to everyone who was there. A few hours later, he returned, to find that another crowd had gathered. He hired them too. He kept returning right through the working day, until the final group who were taken on had to work for little more than an hour or two. The employer was obviously very generous. Too generous – for he paid them all the same wages. Jesus makes the point that they had all agreed their pay in advance, so no one was being cheated. But those who worked all day were not pleased when they saw the others getting the same reward. Now Jesus began that story by saying, "the Kingdom of heaven is like this ..." (Matthew 20:1). God is generous, and longs to give to anyone who is prepared to receive.

Not surprisingly, Jesus met many adults – religious people among them – who were actually incapable of receiving the Kingdom because it did not meet their preconceived expectations of how God should work. Many felt that God's love should be dispensed on a *quid pro quo* basis, and those who were the most righteous should have the first claim on it. But Jesus turned such ideas upside down – and as a result, those who were apparently the least righteous frequently found his message easier to accept.

The decisive point of it all is summed up in Jesus' demand to "repent, and believe in the good news". John the Baptist made a lot of trouble for himself with his demand for repentance, and Jesus found himself facing the same challenge. Many people who were otherwise attracted to what Jesus had to say took it for granted that repentance was something other people should do. People who were Gentiles, perhaps, or "people of the land', or tax gatherers, or people with broken marriages. But surely good upright citizens who were faithful to the traditions of their ancestors had no need of such things. It was an affront to their dignity, not to mention their spiritual achievements, to demand such an about-turn from them. For that is precisely what that word

Mount Arbel, to the west of the Sea of Galilee.

PRAYER

Jesus was always happy mixing with other people. But he was also contented to be by himself. Indeed, he made a point of regularly withdrawing from the crowds who so often followed him, just to spend time alone reflecting on his mission – and in prayer. At key points throughout his life, he found that prayer was an indispensable aid to his own sense of commitment and purpose. After his baptism by John, he spent forty days in the desert, and though he was facing temptations and testing at the time, we can be quite sure that prayer played an important part in that experience. At the end of his life, he withdrew into the Garden of Gethsemane to pray as

he faced the horrors of the cross. And at all points in between, he lived constantly in an atmosphere of prayer – and encouraged his disciples to do the same. Prayer somehow opened the door on a process of spiritual discovery, in which people could reach a new personal maturity as they reflected on life from the perspective of the Kingdom of God that Jesus had come to announce.

Jesus would learn about the importance of prayer from his home and cultural environment. Prayer was of supreme importance in the life of every Jewish family in first century Palestine – just as it is today. One of the most striking

features of the Bible is its insistence that God takes great delight in the prayers of ordinary people. Sometimes prayer would use the conventions of the liturgy – as in the Old Testament book of Psalms. At other times, it was the vehicle through which women and men could share their deepest feelings with God – as Jeremiah and other prophets discovered while agonising about the ministry to which they were called. In Jesus' day, corporate prayer was a part of everyday life for the people of Palestine. The development of local synagogues as places of worship had done much to facilitate this. But prayer was also a regular feature of daily life in the

An oasis in the wilderness of the Judean Desert.

home of the average Jewish family. No doubt Jesus regularly joined with others in this form of worship – when he visited the synagogue, as well as in private homes. Following the pattern of the "benedictions" used in synagogue worship, prayer often focused on God's glory, acknowledged in worship and thanksgiving.

It was Jesus' own example in prayer that led the disciples to ask him to teach them to pray too (Luke 11:1). In response to that, Jesus gave them the pattern of what we now call the Lord's prayer, but which is better described as "the disciples' prayer". This is found in two versions in the gospels – a shorter

Ancient olive trees in the Garden of Gethsemane.

one in Luke (11:2-4) and a more extended one in Matthew (6:9-13). The version in Matthew is the one that is best known, largely because it has a more structured, poetic form, and is easy to remember. Matthew includes it in the Sermon on the Mount, where it integrates with teaching not only about prayer but about other forms of worship as well . Giving money to the poor, prayer, and fasting – these were the three main ways in which Jewish people in the time of Jesus might express their piety. There was nothing wrong with any of them. But it was very easy for them to draw attention to the dedication of the worshipper, rather than to centre on God alone – which is why Jesus not only suggested a form of words which his disciples could use in prayer, but also gave

them some important principles about how they should go about it.

He emphasised that prayer should focus on God. That might seem obvious, but not when you consider those "hypocrites" to whom Jesus referred, standing self-consciously on street corners and praying so that everyone would praise their devotion (Matthew 6:5-6). These "play actors" (for that is the meaning of the Greek word that lies behind the translation "hypocrites") get their reward there and then: everyone applauds when the performance is finished. And that is all the reward they can expect! Jesus made the same point in other ways too. In his story of a Pharisee and a tax collector who went into the temple to pray, the Pharisee as a regular visitor knew all the ropes – and told God so in an eloquent, if ostentatious prayer (Luke 18:9-14). The tax collector, however, was quite unfamiliar with both the ritual and the jargon. All he could do was to acknowledge his own inadequacies before God. Now, asked Jesus, who was in the right with God? His hearers would naturally applaud the religious expert. But it was actually the humble tax collector who put God in first place.

The Lord's Prayer serves as a model in this respect, because it begins by reflecting on God and God's glory, the coming of God's Kingdom – and its challenge – before moving on to the personal concerns of the disciple.

"repent" is all about. It is a demand for an unconditional U-turn, and a radical realignment of a person's entire outlook, in response to what God has done. This declaration of what God has done is "the good news", the gospel.

Jesus explained the nature of this "good news" in many different ways. At an early point in his ministry, he naturally returned to the village where he had spent his childhood and youth. There in the synagogue at Nazareth he was welcomed as a local boy who had made good, and he was invited to read the scriptures on the sabbath day. When he did so, he chose a passage from Isaiah 61:1-2, which had also spoken of the coming of God's "good news". There, the messianic age is described as a time of "good news to the poor", in which God will send a messenger "to proclaim liberty to the captives and recovery of sight to the blind; to set free the oppressed and announce that the time has come when the Lord will save his people". Luke continues by recording that Jesus then said, "This passage of scripture has come true today, as you heard it being read" (Luke 4:16-21).

Actions are clearly identified here as a central element in the coming of God's Kingdom. And Jesus underlined this over and over again in the course of his ministry. When John the Baptist later sent from his prison cell to ask Jesus whether or not he really was the Messiah, the answer that was sent back focused on Jesus' actions. Instead of giving a theologically argued reply, Jesus simply reminded John of what was taking place: "Go back and tell John what you have seen and heard: the blind can see, the lame can walk, the lepers are made clean, the deaf can hear, the dead are raised to life, and the good news is preached to the poor" (Luke 7:22). Matthew and Luke both emphasise that Jesus proclaimed God's Kingdom through deeds as well as words. "Jesus went throughout Galilee, teaching in their synagogues and proclaiming the good news of the kingdom and curing every disease and every sickness among the people" (Matthew 4:23). John for his part describes the miracles of Jesus as "signs", showing the reality of God's presence for all who wanted to see. When the disciples were later sent out, they were commissioned to do exactly the same: "As you go, proclaim the good news, 'The

Spring flowers at Emmaus.

kingdom of heaven has come near.' Cure the sick, raise the dead, cleanse the lepers, cast out demons ... " (Matthew 10:7-8). The teaching of Jesus and the things that he did were just two sides of the same coin. People were attracted to Jesus by his total lifestyle. He himself was the embodiment of the message. He related easily to other people, exuding warmth, generosity and love, because that was the way he thought of God. It was Jesus' constant concern that people should find meaning and fulfilment in life, whatever their needs might be.

Those who are humble enough to become disciples find their relationships with other people can be transformed. They also find a deep inner peace within themselves. But, underlying it all, they discover a new style of relationship with God. Jesus himself referred to God in the familiar way a child would talk of a beloved parent. "Father" was his favourite term to use in prayer. And Jesus encouraged his disciples to use this same intimate address to God. The God of whom he spoke was certainly a transcendent and powerful figure – but not merely a sort of divine essence that

THE FORM OF JESUS' TEACHING

The teachings of Jesus belong in at least two contexts. On the one hand there was the context in the life of Jesus himself: the people to whom he spoke, and the situations in which he lived. But once these teachings were written down in the New Testament gospels, they were also addressing a different audience: the Christian groups for whom the four gospels were written in the middle years of the first century. Even a casual glance through the gospels reveals that each writer used the same basic materials about Jesus to address the issues and concerns of his own day. Mark, for instance, lays great

Good Friday procession at Easter time in Jerusalem.

emphasis on the meaning of discipleship, especially addressing the question of why disciples should suffer persecution. He also emphasises more than the others that Jesus was both Son of God and yet was also an ordinary human being. And fully half of his gospel is taken up with the Passion story, of Jesus' last week of life, his crucifixion and resurrection. No doubt all these features were developed in this way because this enabled Mark to use his material to address the specific concerns of his readers in Rome in the mid-60s of the first century. As a matter of fact, we know this was a time of increasing suffering for Christians under Nero, and it is not at all difficult to see how and why this emphasis should have been so relevant to their needs.

Matthew contains much of the same teaching material as Luke – but the two gospels could hardly be more different in the way they present it. Matthew organised his gospel in a topical way, with easily distinguishable sections dealing with subjects such as ethics, discipleship, parables, the church, and judgment. It is only Matthew who preserves what we call "the Sermon on the Mount" (Matthew 5-7). The same teachings are not missing from Luke, but they appear in different contexts in the story of Jesus. This suggests strongly that it was Matthew who gathered them all together in this particular form – no doubt because that way he could present Jesus to his Jewish readers as a kind of latter-day Moses, delivering a new law for the Kingdom, and calling them to enter into a new covenant with God. That would have meant nothing at all to

Luke's readers, who were upper class Gentiles living in some great city of the Roman empire. Matthew and Luke also often use the same sayings to teach different lessons. For example, in Luke (15:1-7) the story of the lost sheep appears as a parable about people who are outside the Kingdom, and who need to be rescued and brought into its safety. But in Matthew (18:12-14), the same story is applied to those who have been disciples, but have lapsed in their faith and need to be restored.

The gospel of John presents Jesus' teachings in a different way again. It contains nothing comparable with the many parables found in the other three. Though there are still many vivid word pictures, they are mostly about Jesus himself. He is described as the light of the world (8:12), or the door (10:1-18), the good shepherd (10:11) and the true vine (15:1-11). The most frequently used term here is not "the kingdom of God" (which only occurs in 3:3,5 and 18:36,38), but "eternal life" (which features everywhere). In John, Jesus' teaching is mostly delivered in longer, more reflective statements, rather than the kind of short, pithy couplets we find in the other three gospels. John's description of what Jesus did is also different. Certainly there are several miracle stories, some of them quite similar (or even identical) to those in the other gospels. But there are no exorcisms of demons. Nor is there a single mention of tax collectors, who feature so prominently elsewhere.

These differences between the gospels apparently presented no problems for the early church. They were quite happy to accept these four different accounts of Jesus' life and

Rocky outcrop near the garden tomb in Jerusalem, known as Skull Face Rock.

teaching. They were like four portraits of a great leader. No two artists will ever paint exactly the same picture. Jesus was a person to respond to rather than to research and describe in minute historical detail. This apparent freedom to interpret the materials about Jesus has often been felt as an embarrassment by modern Christians. But it is of the essence of what Jesus was about. Throughout all four gospels, there is a strong contrast between Jesus' methods and those of other religious teachers. Rabbis typically insisted that their disciples should learn their teachings off by heart, and then reproduce them exactly. But Jesus was different. He gave his disciples space and creative freedom, to discover themselves as they responded to him. If the early church had insisted on combining the four gospels to

produce just one account, our understanding of Jesus would be much restricted. The fact that they are not quite the same enables modern readers to reflect on Jesus from different angles. And by seeing how his message was able to address the diverse needs of the ancient world, we can see the more clearly how it still has relevance for our own.

pervades all things. The God of whom Jesus spoke was a person, and relating to God is something that happens on a personal level.

LIVING AS DISCIPLES

In the Sermon on the Mount, Jesus emphasised the deep personal care that God has for those who will commit themselves to a life of discipleship. Jesus encouraged his disciples to look at the birds flying around – creatures that trust implicitly in their creator for continuing sustenance and strength – and then reminded them that people are no less valuable in the sight of God. Or, perhaps walking through a meadow as they admired the multicoloured wild flowers all around them, Jesus again pointed out the infinite care that God has for the whole of creation – people included (Matthew 6:25-30).

Jesus also made demands of his disciples. Just as they had taken up the challenge of recognising God's sovereign rule over their lives, so they were to be a living embodiment of that Kingdom, to demonstrate and proclaim its reality in all that they did. Jesus called his disciples to share in the unbelievable generosity of God. A rich man was told, "Sell what you own, and give the money to the poor" (Mark 10:21). Others were exhorted to go two miles if a passing Roman soldier forced them to carry his bags for one (a common experience in occupied Palestine). They should turn the other cheek, and return good for evil (Matthew 5:38-42). All of them, totally absurd things. But the kind of moral absurdity in which God takes delight. For without such extravagance on God's part, who could ever hope to be a part of the Kingdom?

Much of Jesus' teaching centres on the relationship of individuals to the Kingdom of God. But there is also a strong emphasis on the value of the corporate life of God's people. When asked, Jesus made it plain that one of the two great commandments was that women and men should love their neighbour as themselves – and one of the most striking of all the parables was told in response to the question, "Who is my neighbour?" The story of the good Samaritan stretched the concept of serving others almost to breaking point (Luke 10:29-37). But Jesus also demanded that his followers should display

CAN WE TRUST THE GOSPELS?

Apart from the New Testament, only two or three other ancient sources even mention Jesus at all. When they do, they give us virtually no specific facts about him (though many Latin and Greek writers do of course

An ancient stepped street in Jerusalem, on the probable route from the Garden of Gethsemane after Jesus' arrest.

document the activities of his followers later in the first century). If the New Testament gospels are not reasonably reliable records of who Jesus was and what he said and did, then we can know nothing at all about him. So can we trust them?

Much time and effort has been expended over the years by scholars and experts trying to answer this question. No one has plausibly

concluded that Jesus never actually existed, so we can be sure of that much at least. But the opinions of the experts vary widely. At one extreme, it has been argued that Jesus followed the practice of other Jewish rabbis by insisting that his disciples learn his teachings off by heart – and that these sayings were then written down to become the gospels. At the opposite extreme, some have suggested that since the gospels were written by Christians living outside of Palestine at least a

generation later than the events they report, we should treat them with a great deal of caution, if not scepticism. And yet others have argued that it really does not matter anyway, because true Christian faith should not be made to depend on "proving" things rationally. Real faith cannot be subject to proof, they imply, and if it could then where would the element of faith come in? So on this understanding, it could actually be an impediment to know too much about the historical Jesus!

All these positions involve complex and tortuous arguments, and space does not allow us to enter into a detailed engagement with them here. Instead, we can review the evidence and leave readers to form their own conclusions. What, then, are the facts which we should take into account?

1 It is certain that neither Jesus nor any of his immediate close associates wrote down either his story or his teachings during the course of his lifetime. The gospels were not written before the mid-40s at the earliest, and in the view of many experts they were written much later. They were also written in Greek, whereas we assume that Jesus normally delivered his teachings in Aramaic. At best, therefore, what we now have must be translations from one language into another. As a matter of fact, this argument is less compelling today than it once seemed to be, for not only do we know that Jesus probably spoke Greek, but some of his teachings were almost certainly originally delivered in that language. For instance, the saying about giving to Caesar what is Caesar's (Mark 12: 17) almost certainly refers to the Greek inscription on a coin of

Tiberius's reign bearing the word "Caesar" (for which there was no Aramaic equivalent). Other gospel passages (e.g. John 21) also use word plays which would mean nothing in Aramaic. At the same time, the gospels also preserve Aramaic words transliterated into Greek. Words like *Amen*, *Abba*, or even at times whole phrases (e.g. *Talitha koum*, Mark 5:41). And in many more instances Aramaic ways of constructing sentences have been shown to lie behind the writings of the gospels in Greek. Much of Jesus' teaching in the Sermon on the Mount, for instance, forms perfect Aramaic poetic couplets when translated out of Greek back into that language. None of this actually proves that Jesus said these words, but it does anchor the gospel records into the sort of world in which we know Jesus must have lived. Since this world was significantly different from that of the gospel writers, who lived mostly in the western empire and would be familiar only with Greek and Latin, then if they use phrases and constructions related to Aramaic, that at least implies they were depending on source materials whose origins were firmly rooted in Palestinian culture.

2 The gospel writers were all Christians who were wrestling with the big issues that gripped the Christian church in the middle to the end of the first century. At least part of their purpose in writing about Jesus was to relate his life and teachings to the concerns of their own churches. They were not simply writing history for its own sake. This fact has sometimes led people to suppose that the gospel writers made

no distinction between their own teachings and what they claimed Jesus had said. But in fact, there are some striking differences between what we know to have been major concerns of the early Christian communities and what we find in the gospels. The question of if, and on what terms, Jews and Gentiles should relate to one another was a major debate within these early churches. It would have been highly convenient if Jesus could have been made to say something about whether Gentile Christians should be circumcised and keep the Old Testament Law, for example. If the gospel writers were accustomed to inventing sayings of Jesus, there must have been an overwhelming temptation for them to include something on this burning issue. The fact is that it never features anywhere at all. Nor for that matter do any of the early church's favourite titles for Jesus. Lord, Son of God, Saviour – these were the names most frequently applied to Jesus later on. But in the gospels, he is consistently called "Son of Man" – a term that appears only once elsewhere in the New Testament, and then not in any of its central theological documents (Acts 7:56). The same thing is true of subjects like baptism, which very early became the rite of admission into the church – but never features at all in either Jesus' teaching or practice. The gospel writers appear to have been conscious that, notwithstanding their desire to address the readers of their own day by means of their stories of Jesus, this still did not give them permission simply to manufacture new sayings of Jesus at will. In his own discussion of a subject which Jesus did talk about

information in the gospels that shows a writer must have had access to highly authentic data. John, for example, was once thought to be a sentimental account of Jesus' teachings bearing little relation to the facts. But we now know this is a mistaken judgment. Not only is John very deeply rooted in Jewish and Aramaic traditions, but it also describes with great accuracy places in Jerusalem that were destroyed long before the gospel itself was written.

The process whereby the gospels were written was a complex interaction between the original stories of Jesus, going right back in oral history to the time of Jesus himself, and the concern of the gospel writers to address the needs of their readers. But there is no evidence to suggest that they allowed these needs to override the importance of reporting what Jesus said and did as accurately as they could. We may not have all the answers – and particular questions need to be addressed on their own merits – but we can be quite sure that the New Testament portraits of Jesus give us an accurate enough impression of who he was, what he did, and what he taught.

(marriage), the Christian leader Paul went out of his way to make a distinction between what were his own opinions and what he called "words of the Lord" (1 Corinthians 7). We have no reason to doubt that other Christians exercised the same care. As a matter of fact, if we tried to reconstruct what was going on in the early church from the materials available to us in the gospels, the picture we could produce would bear no relation to the facts as we know them.

3 At the same time, we need to remember that the gospels are not biographies – at least not in our modern sense of the word. Only two of them mention Jesus' birth, none of them say anything about his life as a young adult, only Luke records one incident from his childhood, and much of the focus of all four is on the events of the final week of his life. All of them put together do not contain enough material to document three years of anyone's life, let alone someone as active as Jesus obviously was. These are clearly selective accounts, with different incidents being selected according to the purpose of the various writers – purposes that at least two of them actually identify (Luke 1:1-4, John 20:31). This is why we have not one agreed account in the New Testament, but four different gospels. The writers were following the customs of ancient biographers, trying to show how the lessons of one person's life and activities could relate to the diverse circumstances of their various readers. Though their methods are different from our own, ancient writers generally took no less trouble to check their sources than their modern counterparts would. Writers like Thucydides or Lucian were neither fools nor frauds, and Luke at least clearly claims to be working within the same kind of historical procedures as they were. Quite often, we come across the same qualities of loving self-sacrifice in their dealings with one another. He went further, and told them that the nature of their own group would play a key role in attracting others to the Kingdom of God: "I give you a new commandment, that you love one another. Just as I have loved you, you also should love one another. By this everyone will know that you are my disciples, if you have love for one another" (John 13:34-35).

This emphasis on sharing the good news with others runs like a golden thread through the entire fabric of the gospel stories. Jesus does not call disciples merely to find fulfilment for themselves – though he does offer that. Nor does he offer them an

"SECRET" GOSPELS

In our account of Jesus' teachings, we have taken our information from the four New Testament gospels of Matthew, Mark, Luke and John. But do they actually portray the real Jesus? Are there other sources of information that might give us a different picture?

There certainly were other so-called "gospels" circulating in the early centuries of the Christian era, and some people have claimed they give a more authentic picture of Jesus, which is why we need to give some attention to them here. They date from the third and fourth centuries, and their existence has been known for a long time. Leaders in the ancient church occasionally mentioned such "gospels" in their own writings, usually identifying them as the work of a group called "Gnostics". But it is only in modern times that actual copies have come to light, especially with the discovery of a substantial collection of such writings just after the Second World War.

Isolated fragments had been known for some time, but it was towards the end of 1945, as a camel driver by the name of Mohammed Ali El-Samman was digging for manure at the foot of the cliffs of Gebel et Tarif, not far from the modern town of Nag Hammadi in upper Egypt, that the most spectacular finds came to light. While he was scooping up the decomposed bird droppings to use on his farm, Mohammed uncovered a large jar. Inside, he found a collection of papyrus leaves, bound like books between leather covers. They were in Coptic – a language he did not understand – so he took them along to the priest of the local Coptic church. He was also unable to read them, as they were in an ancient form of the language which he did not know. After long and complex black market dealings,

View across the River Nile at Nag Hammadi, Egypt.

these documents eventually fell into the possession of scholars, who identified them as the remains of the library of an ancient monastic community. The manuscripts had names like "The Gospel of Philip", "The Gospel of Thomas", "The Gospel of Truth", and others even more esoteric. Circumstantial evidence suggested they had been bound about AD 350, and hidden away not long after that.

So do these "gospels" contain an alternative message of Jesus – perhaps even his "real" teaching, which was disowned for some reason by the leaders of the early church and had lain unread until their discovery in modern times? Claims of this sort are being made with increasing frequency today.

Not everything that Jesus said found its way into the New Testament gospels. Luke and John both tell us that they took their stories from much larger collections known to them (Luke 1:1-4, John 20:30, 21:25). So in principle there is no particular reason why some of this other material should not have survived elsewhere. It would be surprising if it had not. The Gospel of Thomas contains 114 sayings of Jesus. Most of Thomas is quite plainly a Gnostic reinterpretation of the sayings. But some of them do seem to reflect older traditions. There is a story of how a wise fisherman caught many fish. Most of them were too small to be any use, but he found one large fish and kept it. It is not difficult to see the similarities between this and the story of the pearls told in Matthew 13:45-6. This is a very typical case. The vast majority of these other sayings are very similar to well-known New Testament passages. But they are generally not identical, because they are then applied and explained in accordance with the beliefs of the Gnostic group who apparently collected them in this form.

So does Thomas contain expansions and additions? Or is it the New Testament gospels that have serious omissions? If we could be sure that Thomas was compiled as early as some of the New Testament gospels, then that would be a

easy ride – though he assures them that their burdens can become lighter as they follow him closely (Matthew 11:29-30). But everywhere, he calls them to share what they have discovered with others who are still searching for spiritual meaning in life.

"GO INTO ALL THE WORLD"

Jesus' teaching on the importance of sharing the faith with others has frequently been abused, as Christians have perceived it to be an open invitation to imperialistic exploitation. Of course, it is nothing of the sort. In a striking exhortation delivered after the resurrection, Jesus instructed his disciples, "As the Father has sent me, so I send you" (John 20:21). Jesus was predominantly a figure of weakness. Yet paradoxically, it was in his very weakness that the true strength of his message was to be found. It was in the ultimate act of giving himself totally for humankind on the cross that God's Kingdom finally and decisively burst into the world. And when Jesus came to send his disciples out at the end of the story, they were told to go as he himself had come: not from a position of power, but of powerlessness.

Matthew's "Great Commission" seems a fitting conclusion to

genuine question. As it is, Thomas in its present form seems to date from about the fourth century, and no one doubts that it is a thoroughly Gnostic text. Some of its sayings are found in the New Testament, in a slightly different form, and when we compare them it is obvious that the sayings in Thomas are a development based on the New Testament, and not some form of "independent" – still less "more reliable" – gospel. Claims that Thomas or any other Gnostic gospels contain the "real teaching" of Jesus are nothing more than imagination and wishful thinking.

The truth is that the Gnostics amended the sayings of Jesus to give credence to their own outlook. They believed that personal fulfilment and salvation were found through union with some kind of cosmic consciousness, and the way to access this was barred to all but a few, who happened to have the appropriate secret "knowledge" (the meaning of the Greek word *gnosis*). Not surprisingly, Jesus then appears in these alternative "gospels" as a teacher of such secrets. He is also usually only a semi-human being, who offers a salvation that is world-denying and can only be enjoyed in some other spiritual place. This is quite different from the Jesus of the New Testament, whose message brought hope to people in the midst of life in this world. He spoke of God not as some remote figure, but as the creator, who was deeply involved in the affairs of everyday life. And as his disciples reflected on his message, they were quite sure that salvation was not a matter of escaping from the world, but meeting God in it – especially in the life, death and resurrection of Jesus, whom they perceived to be both fully divine and fully human.

Jesus' teaching (Matthew 28:16-20), and it sums up in a succinct way so much that is distinctive about Jesus. "Go", Jesus tells them. They are not to expect other people to come and ask them about their message. Instead, they are to take it to where others are to be found. Jesus always met people on their own territory, where they felt safe, but he was potentially vulnerable. Nor were they to go with false confidence to share this good news, but rather as people who themselves had doubts (Matthew 28:17). They had something worth sharing with others, not because they themselves were different from other people, but because they were no different.

Jesus also commissioned them to "make disciples". Their aim should be to enrol people as students, learners alongside a teacher. Just as Jesus had invited his own disciples to join him as equals ("friends", John 15:15), so they were to reach out to others – not lording it over them as if they had all the answers, but recognising that they too still had much to learn about life in God's Kingdom (Mark 10:41-45). This was clearly in mind when Jesus mentioned the need for "teaching": becoming and being a disciple was not a once-for-all action, but a lifelong commitment.

The theme of two of the shortest parables underlines this. "The kingdom of heaven is like treasure hidden in a field", said Jesus, "which someone found and hid; then in his joy he goes and sells all that he has and buys that field. Again, the kingdom of heaven is like a merchant in search of fine pearls; on finding one pearl of great value, he went and sold all that he had and bought it" (Matthew 13:44-5). The worst fate imaginable is to be shut out of God's Kingdom – which is why it is worth giving up everything to follow Jesus.

CRUCIFIXION & RESURRECTION

FROM GALILEE TO JERUSALEM

IT WAS in Galilee that Jesus felt most at home. This was where he had grown up as a boy, and this was where he recruited his disciples. Though some rejected him, most Galileans responded warmly to what he had to say.

But Galilee was not the centre of Judaism, and eventually Jesus had to leave Galilee for the last time, and head for Jerusalem. He had visited the city before, of course, and may have gone regularly to celebrate the great Jewish festivals in the temple. The only New Testament story of his childhood shows him during a pilgrimage to Jerusalem with Mary and Joseph, engaging in theological debates with the rabbis (Luke 2:41-52). On that occasion they were amazed by his understanding – as well they might have been, for a boy of twelve was not yet considered old enough to observe the Old Testament Law, let alone discuss its finer points with religious experts. As the true nature of Jesus'

Jewish boy holds the Torah message gradually unfolded during the years that
at his Bar Mitzvah followed, astonishment turned into alarm, and

alarm into outright opposition.

Long before the end of his three-year teaching ministry, Jesus knew he would meet some stiff opposition from the religious leaders of his nation. Arguably, that was why he spent so much time in Galilee: the people there had a more open-minded attitude towards religious affairs, and were temperamentally more likely to be interested in the novel views of a new teacher. But what happened in Jerusalem during the final week of Jesus' life is central to understanding his entire ministry. Almost a half of Mark's gospel is devoted to just these few days. Mark describes a time of increasing tension between Jesus and the religious authorities, culminating eventually in his arrest, trial, and crucifixion.

It is easy to get the impression that Jesus was contriving a

ROMANS AND JEWS

When Herod the Great died in 4 BC, both the country and his own family were left in chaos. The semi-independence of Judea was at an end, for though Herod left a will, it was subject to the approval of Augustus, who naturally divided the country up as he pleased. Behind the scenes, Rome had always been the real ruler of Palestine since Pompey's invasion in 63 BC, but with Herod's death it asserted its sovereignty more directly.

Herod's son Antipas disputed the terms of the will, and along with his brothers Archelaus and Philip, was called to Rome to see the emperor. While this consultation was taking place, the whole country was torn apart by revolts, all of which were crushed by Roman troops. Augustus decided that in the circumstances it made sense to divide Palestine between the three of them. Archelaus got Samaria, Judea and Idumea, while the rest was split between Philip and Antipas.

This was a compromise arrangement. Had Augustus given the kingdom intact to any of the three, it could easily have provoked all-out war. Yet to introduce direct Roman government would have incensed the Zealots and other nationalists. In the event, Archelaus proved to be so incompetent that even the longstanding rivalry between Jews and Samaritans was laid aside so they could present a united complaint about him to Augustus. As a result, in AD 6 Archelaus was recalled to Rome, and sent off into exile in Gaul. Augustus could have appointed one of the other two brothers in his place, but he knew that whoever was not appointed would almost certainly plot the downfall of his brother. In any case, he really trusted neither of them, and so Quirinius, the imperial legate of Syria, was sent to take a census of the taxable property of Judea, as the first stage in its organisation as a province within the Roman empire.

Judea became one of the imperial provinces of the empire, and was governed by a procurator of equestrian rank, a man called Coponius. We know very little about how these procurators were allowed to govern their provinces. Indeed, there is some doubt as to whether they should be called "procurators" at all. Tacitus certainly applied this title to Pontius Pilate, but there is some evidence that "prefect" was the correct title at the time. In *The Jewish War*, Josephus states that Coponius "was entrusted by Augustus with full powers and authority to inflict the death penalty" (2.117) – which seems to imply that the governor had the equivalent of the imperium exercised by the proconsuls in other parts of the empire. There is no ancient definition of what this imperium amounted to, but it apparently deliberate confrontation with the leaders of the nation. By going to Jerusalem, he would challenge them in the most forthright way possible, and provoke them into action. But the gospels present a more sophisticated perspective. Despite all that had gone before, Jesus still had a genuine compassion for the religious institutions and their leaders, and a heartfelt attachment to his nation: "Jerusalem, Jerusalem, the city that kills the prophets and stones those who are sent to it! How often have I desired to gather your children together as a hen gathers her brood under her wings, and you were not willing!" (Luke 12:34). Jesus loved his people, he respected their long and ancient spiritual heritage – and he wanted them to rediscover God's loving guidance in their lives at this crucial juncture of their history. But he also knew their track record. Even the leading prophets of Old Testament times had

conferred supreme power in administration, defence, the dispensation of justice, and the maintenance of public order.

The maintenance of order would certainly be a major concern in a province like Judea, with such a volatile population in a strategic position on the edge of the empire. As a judge, the procurator had absolute authority in matters of life and death within his province, and even Roman citizens could appeal to Caesar only in special circumstances. Very few cases would actually come to the procurator. Most minor affairs would be settled in the various local courts, or in the Jerusalem Sanhedrin where Jewish law was properly understood and dispensed. Only crimes involving capital punishment would be referred to the procurator, since he was the only one with power to prescribe the death sentence. The Sanhedrin was concerned with matters relating to traditional Jewish law, in civil and criminal cases, as well as matters relating to religion. In Judea, it

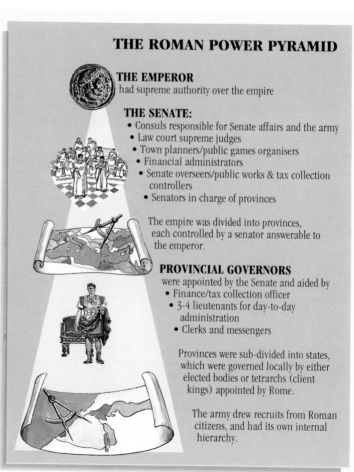

THE ROMAN POWER PYRAMID

THE EMPEROR
had supreme authority over the empire

THE SENATE:
- Consuls responsible for Senate affairs and the army
- Law court supreme judges
- Town planners/public games organisers
- Financial administrators
- Senate overseers/public works & tax collection controllers
- Senators in charge of provinces

The empire was divided into provinces, each controlled by a senator answerable to the emperor.

PROVINCIAL GOVERNORS
were appointed by the Senate and aided by
- Finance/tax collection officer
- 3-4 lieutenants for day-to-day administration
- Clerks and messengers

Provinces were sub-divided into states, which were governed locally by either elected bodies or tetrarchs (client kings) appointed by Rome.

The army drew recruits from Roman citizens, and had its own internal hierarchy.

been rejected. In one of the final parables recorded in the gospels (Mark 12:1-12), Jesus compared the nation Israel to a vineyard, carefully cultivated by its owner, and then let out to tenants. When the owner sent his servants to collect a share of the harvests, they were regularly beaten up or even killed. Eventually, the owner sent his son, supposing he would be given more respect. But he too was killed. All the gospels insist that from an early stage in his ministry, Jesus knew this would be the way he would meet his death.

SUFFERING AND GLORY

This was a disagreeable concept for the disciples, and even leading lights such as Peter, James and John never fully understood what Jesus was saying on the subject. But the gospel

could make arrests, try and condemn criminals to any punishment apart from death, without any recourse to the procurator – though on occasion this prescription was ignored, and mobs took matters into their own hands by lynching criminals after only a Jewish trial.

The procurator's court would be formally run, with charges being presented against the accused by any private parties with an interest in the case. There was no inquisition by the court, and cases were heard by the holder of the imperium on his tribunal, generally assisted by his consilium of friends and officials, who constituted a panel of reference rather than a jury. All these features can be found in the trial of Jesus.

There was a whole network of local courts to deal with other matters. Judea was divided into eleven toparchies, or districts, and each village within a toparchy had its own council, presided over by a village clerk. They would deal with civil cases and certain less important

criminal ones. Since this was the official structure of the land, it is surprising to find no reference to it in the gospels. Neither village clerks nor the commandants who controlled each toparchy feature in the gospels, though the tax collectors who do would be part of the same system of administration. At a time when their independence was suspended, it was natural for Jews to want to use their own ancient procedures, even if it had only a theoretical significance. As a result, the authority of the village congregation, the rulers of the synagogue, was widely respected, even though it had no officially recognised jurisdiction.

We know little of the way that Philip and Antipas organised things, except that their territories did not fall under the jurisdiction of the procurators. They had the right to mint their own coins, and Philip went so far as to put his own head on them – a thoroughly un-Jewish action. But the area he ruled was

well away from the mainstream of Jewish life. Antipas was the local ruler of Galilee, which is why Pilate sent Jesus to him for trial. Maybe he hoped that there would be some loophole in the law of Galilee that would enable Antipas to take responsibility for a citizen of his own territory. But Jesus had already described this same Antipas as a "fox" (Luke 13:32), and he was certainly far too crafty to allow himself to be duped in this way. As a result of his clever manoeuvring on this and other issues, he managed to stay in power until AD 39, long after Pilate had been removed from office.

*Scene of Jesus'
transfiguration: Mount
Hermon from the south.*

writers go out of their way to emphasise that the cross was not a mistake. Even such apparently undeserved suffering was an integral part of God's plan. Christian faith is not about the exercise of brute force. On the contrary, true power is found in those whom the world rejects as worthless – whether Jesus, or the marginalised group who were his disciples.

Mark introduces the final stage of Jesus' ministry with the story of the transfiguration (Mark 9:2-13). This has no place in John's gospel, where Jesus is unhesitatingly portrayed as the divine Son of God right from the very beginning. But in the other gospels, he is more often described as the "Son of Man", with all the ambiguity implied in that title. Yet even here, a few episodes show Jesus as an altogether more celestial being. The transfiguration is one, but there is also the voice which spoke at Jesus' baptism (Mark 1:9-11) – and, in Luke's story, the ascension (Luke 24:50-53, Acts 1:6-11). Many Old Testament passages had described God's presence as a bright shining light, and for a brief moment on a mountain top it all focused on Jesus. For those with the eyes (or faith) to see, it was a glimpse of the coming kingdom in all its splendour and glory – an impression that must have been heightened by the appearance of Moses and Elijah alongside Jesus. According to Jewish tradition, these two heroes did not die, but were caught up direct to the presence of God. Both of them were associated with messianic expectations. The end times had been connected to the arrival of "a prophet like Moses" (Deuteronomy 18:18-20), while Elijah had been identified as the forerunner of the Messiah himself (Malachi 4:5) – a forerunner whom many thought had already come in the person of John the Baptist.

The whole scene recalls several Old Testament passages. The high mountain, the shining of Jesus' face, and the cloud which covered God's glory – all these elements had played a central part when Moses received the Law on Mount Sinai (Exodus 19:16, 24:15-18, 34:29-35). The mention of building booths or "tabernacles" also seems to recall the celebration of the

Pathway down through the Kidron Valley to the city of Jerusalem.

annual Feast of Tabernacles. At this time, temporary tents were built to commemorate the time Israel's ancestors spent in the wilderness. This was one of the most important festivals in Jesus' day: as well as directing the people to their past, it also reminded them that one day Israel's fortunes would be restored. But while the Law had traditionally been the way to understand God's will, now the voice from heaven was proclaiming that it was Jesus whose message should be taken seriously. The words are similar to those spoken previously at his baptism, and no doubt pick up some of the themes implied there. In particular, coming so immediately after the story of Peter's confession of Jesus as Messiah and Mark's explanation of how the Son of Man would suffer and die, it emphasises that this understanding of messiahship was nothing new, but was consistent with God's will down through the ages.

Mark never identifies the precise location of any of his stories, and this one is no exception. But some clues in the narrative seem to imply it took place on Mount Hermon, the highest point in the land (Mount Sinai was much further south). Cyril of Jerusalem later suggested the transfiguration actually took place on Mount Tabor, which is only 9 kilometres south east of Nazareth, and about 16 kilometres from the Sea of Galilee. This is an easier mountain for pilgrims to climb, which no doubt encouraged such an identification. But Mark 9:14 also suggests that when Jesus and his closest friends came down from the mountain they found the rest of the disciples talking with "scribes". Mount Hermon was in a pagan region, and it is less likely that Jewish teachers would readily be found there. On the other hand, the exact location of the transfiguration is unimportant. In the overall context of the gospel story of Jesus' life, it serves as a transition from the earlier episodes in Galilee, to the final opposition that ultimately led to the cross.

GOING UP TO JERUSALEM

Shortly after this incident, Jesus set off on his final journey to Jerusalem. Again, the geographical details are unclear. Matthew (19:1) and Mark (10:1) both mention Jesus crossing over to the eastern side of the river Jordan, while Luke (9:52) writes of a

journey through Samaria. On the basis of such information, it is impossible to plot Jesus' route. But then, the gospel writers were not generally

The Jordan River near Banyas (Caesarea Philippi), in the far north.

interested in geography, and in this particular case they may have left the details deliberately vague in order to depict this as a time when Jesus took the chance to reinforce and summarise his earlier teaching, so the disciples would be well grounded in it once he was taken from them. Luke in particular includes much of Jesus' teaching at this point in his story.

On the way to Jerusalem, Jesus came to the city of Jericho. Jericho was a good place to live. The climate, the soil, and the ready availability of water all guaranteed that. It is the oldest continuously inhabited city on earth, dating as far back as 9000 BC, and several key events in the history of Israel had taken place in and around this city. Like many other settlements, it suffered a decline in its fortunes at the time of the Jewish exile, some 500 years before the time of Christ. But by New Testament times it was enjoying a renaissance. Herod the Great built a palace and a theatre in the neighbourhood, along with new aqueducts to irrigate the area.

Luke comments that Jesus "set his face to go to Jerusalem" (Luke 9:51) – a term that indicates total commitment, single-mindedness and determination. So by the time he got to Jericho, Jesus must have been preoccupied with what was going to happen when he eventually got to Jerusalem. But he still had time for other people. At Jericho, he healed a blind man (named Bartimaeus in Mark 10:46-52), and called yet another disciple. This time it was Zacchaeus, a tax collector, who gave Jesus hospitality in his home. Zacchaeus was apparently a small man,

Bedouin tents on the route between Jericho and Jerusalem.

who needed to climb a tree to see Jesus over the heads of the crowd who were following him. Modern visitors to Jericho can still see what is claimed to be the tree (though today's city is located well to the east of the town Jesus knew!). But Zacchaeus is remembered for more than that. As a result of this encounter with Jesus, his entire lifestyle was radically changed. He voluntarily returned the proceeds of his professional extortion fourfold (twice what the Law demanded), and gave half his possessions to the poor (Luke 19:1-10).

JESUS ON TRIAL

Who was it who actually conspired to bring about the death of Jesus? What was the precise relationship between the various Jewish leaders who feature in the gospel stories, and the Roman Pontius Pilate who eventually condemned Jesus? That may sound like the sort of historical conundrum that would interest only a minority of people. But in reality it has been one of the hottest subjects in discussion of Jesus' death for many generations. Down through the centuries, the belief that the Jews were responsible for the crucifixion of Jesus has led to the most horrific persecution of that nation. Even the Nazi holocaust can, in some respects, be traced back to religious roots. Reading many of the books written by leading Bible scholars in pre-war Germany, it is not difficult to see how

their apparently abstruse historical and theological theories actually gave encouragement to those who for political and racial reasons already hated the Jewish people. The claim that Judaism was a dead and lifeless religion, designed only to keep people in bondage rather than setting them free to live life to the full, can only have fuelled the fires of anti-semitism that swept across Europe in the 1930s. And the certainty that Jewish leaders were in the vanguard of the opposition to

DEATH AND RESURRECTION

	THURSDAY	FRIDAY	SATURDAY	SUNDAY
Morning		Accused before Pilate. Before Herod. Pilate offers to release Jesus. Condemned. Judas commits suicide. Soldiers mock Jesus. Crucified. Preparation for Passover.	Sabbath Passover	Jesus resurrected, appears to Mary.
Afternoon		Jesus dies.		Jesus appears to two on Emmaus road.
Evening	Last Supper. Jesus arrested, Disciples flee. Jesus before Annas. Jesus before Caiaphas and Jewish Council.	Jesus' body removed from cross and laid in tomb. Sabbath begins. Passover begins.		Jesus appears to the disciples in the upper room.

The road from Jericho to Jerusalem is a steep climb. It begins at about 260 metres below sea level, and climbs to something like 770 metres above it. The route followed by Jesus would be slightly to the north of the present highway, and in his day was little more than a dirt track (though it was later paved by the Romans).

JERUSALEM AT LAST

Jesus and his companions entered Jerusalem through Bethany and Bethphage, and then went on to the Mount of Olives (Mark

Jesus merely fanned the flames to even greater intensity.

So what is the truth? Right away, it has to be said that the New Testament nowhere suggests that either Jews or Romans should carry all the blame, in any absolute sense. At one time, it can seem as if "the residents of Jerusalem and their leaders" were instrumental in Jesus' death (Acts 13:27). At another, Judas or Pilate, or the devil, or other cosmic forces (1 Corinthians 2:7-8). The fact is that the precise identity of the players in this drama is not all that important. The kind of goodness represented by Jesus makes us all uncomfortable, and most of us would have reacted to him in exactly the same way as his contemporaries did. In any case, the New Testament sees Jesus' death in a broader perspective, as part of God's plan to redeem humankind from an existence of misery.

At first sight, the gospels appear to describe at least two trials of Jesus: one before the high priest Caiaphas, at which charges were formulated in terms of Jewish religious law, and the other before Pilate, at which these religious charges were changed to become political accusations under Roman law. In understanding exactly what was going on, we are hampered by our complete lack of information about Jewish legal customs and practices at the time of Jesus. The Mishnah contains regulations formulated about AD 200, which certainly developed in a previous generation, though perhaps not as early as the first century. Judged by these later standards, the kind of "trial" described in the gospels would certainly have been very irregular. The leading members of the Sanhedrin were both prosecution and judges, and they had already been involved in plotting to have Jesus arrested. The trial opened with no specific charges against Jesus, and no evidence was called for the defence, even when the prosecution witnesses disagreed. In addition, two crucial rules of later Jewish law were ignored completely. These laid down that 24 hours had to elapse between a death sentence and its execution; and that a trial should not be held on the day before the sabbath. If these rules were in operation at the time, then what happened to Jesus can be made to look highly irregular. But that is unlikely. For one thing, the members of the Sanhedrin were not rogues: they were people of high moral ideals and considerable integrity. Moreover, they were genuinely convinced that Jesus was wrong, and acted in accordance with their own religious perceptions. It has to be significant that, of all the complaints the early Christians directed against the Jews, they never accused them of acting illegally in order to get rid of Jesus.

The various investigations before Annas and Caiaphas were probably informal enquiries, held for the purpose of establishing the facts of the case. Since the Jews had no power to impose a death sentence themselves, there would be no point in holding a formal trial. Only the Romans could sentence a man to death, which means that Pilate's role was central. Crucifixion was a distinctively Roman form of punishment, and in the end of the day, it was Pilate's vacillation and weakness of character that resulted in Jesus dying there.

11:1). From here, Jesus made a rather stylish entry to the city. He sent some disciples to one of the nearby villages, telling them where they *Ancient olive tree at Bethany, near Jerusalem.* would find a colt tied up, on which he planned to ride into the capital. There is no hint as to how Jesus knew about the animal. Perhaps he had some kind of supernatural knowledge, or maybe he simply had friends there whose generosity he could rely on. Presumably Jesus had travelled on foot this far, and the introduction of a mount into the drama was a new and significant development. Kings often commandeered horses to carry them, and there was a popular expectation that the Messiah would ride on a stallion up to the temple mount, and there proclaim the coming of God's kingdom. Some of those who were accompanying Jesus certainly identified his actions with such predictions. Many of them had come all the way from Galilee just for this very moment, and they instinctively took up positions as if they were the regular retinue of an oriental monarch. Some laid their clothes on the colt to make a saddle, while others threw their coats on the ground before Jesus. They tore down palm branches, and joined in an enthusiastic rendition of some words from Psalm 118:

Hosanna
Blessed is the one who comes in the name of the Lord!
Blessed is the coming kingdom of our ancestor David!
Hosanna in the highest heaven!

Christians have always celebrated this event on Palm Sunday, just one week before Easter. But some believe it could have taken place a good while before Jesus' last days. Jesus' crucifixion was at Passover time, in the spring. But palm branches were a distinctive feature of Tabernacles, which was in the autumn. Then, the worshippers carried such branches and waved them high every time the word "Hosanna" was spoken in the liturgy. Could it be that Mark reduced the time scale in order to highlight the significant elements in the growing conflict between Jesus and the authorities? Certainly, Jesus later commented that "Day after day I was with you teaching in the Temple ... " (14:49), which may suggest a much longer ministry at this point than a week or less. On the other hand, Psalm 118 was one of the "Hallel" psalms (113-118), which were a common feature of Passover celebrations. And spreading clothes or branches in the path of a hero could easily have been a spontaneous gesture. Centuries before, the Israelite Jehu had been acclaimed as king in this way (2 Kings 9:13), while nearer to Jesus' own day, the conquering hero Simon Maccabaeus had been welcomed to Jerusalem not only with waving branches, but with singing as well (1 Maccabees 13:51).

The Hebrew word "Hosanna" is literally a prayer, meaning "Lord save us", though it could also be used more casually as an expression of spiritual fervour and praise. But the words "the one who comes in the name of the Lord" could only refer to some sort of messianic figure, and suggests that Jesus' companions were consciously welcoming the king to his capital. The story in John certainly suggests this (12:13), while Matthew observes that by arriving in this way Jesus was fulfilling a messianic prophecy found in Zechariah 9:9 (Matthew 21:5). In the light of all that had gone before, the messianic atmosphere of the whole event must have been obvious, if paradoxical. For unlike the Messiah of legend and mythology, Jesus did not arrive on a war horse, but on a donkey. Moreover, Jesus did not take the temple by storm. Entering the temple area from the south through the Huldah Gate (now blocked up), he merely took a look around before returning to Bethany to spend the night. When he first began his ministry with John's baptism, the voice from heaven spoke in words that evoked Old Testament images of both majesty and suffering. Now, as Jesus entered his final week, the two themes were brought together once more.

THE FINAL SHOWDOWN

Jesus did return to the temple, of course, and his forthright comments on the way it was being abused led to the final showdown with the authorities. As he threw the money-changers out

Palm Sunday procession at Bethphage, on the approach to Jerusalem.

of the temple, his words were very similar to the way Jeremiah had condemned the nation centuries before – and those with a sense of history got the message (Mark 11:15-17). Jesus seemed to be declaring that unless the nation changed its ways, then God would bring a judgment as severe as the exile, and even the temple itself would not be spared.

Not surprisingly, the leaders of the nation felt they had to take action. The triumphal entry into Jerusalem, accompanied by a large crowd, then followed by such autocratic behaviour in the temple, could only mean one thing: Jesus was planning a revolution. As Jesus continued to teach, it was not long before he had provided enough evidence to allow formal action to be taken against him. As he mixed with the crowds in the streets and the temple, he was repeatedly asked on whose authority he was acting. On one occasion, he compared himself with John the Baptist, who was widely regarded as a prophet sent from God (Mark 11:27-33). At another time he appeared to question the authority of the emperor, by replying to a question about tax paying with the words, "pay the emperor what belongs to the emperor, and pay God what belongs to God" (Mark 12:17). From this point onwards, Jesus' popular support began to disappear. The very idea of ever paying anything to the emperor was bad news for those who wanted a political deliverer. But to suggest there were some things the emperor should never be given was good news for those who were looking for a political charge they could bring against him.

Jesus continued teaching for one or two more days yet, but there is no further mention of large crowds following him. Even one of his own disciples – Judas Iscariot – deserted him, at the very time when the rest of them were meeting for their last meal together. This was on the Thursday night of Holy Week – Passover night, according to Mark's calculations. The Passover was traditionally celebrated in the home. So many pilgrims came to Jerusalem from all over the world, that those who lived there had to make rooms available to visitors so they could celebrate the Passover meal within the boundaries of the city itself (boundaries which were themselves specially extended so as to accommodate as many as possible!). Jesus sent two disciples to find a suitable room for the purpose.

"Follow a man carrying a jar of water", he said. Carrying water was always a woman's job, so even with the city crowded for the festival, a man would not be difficult to spot. But the main emphasis is not on the place, but the words that Jesus spoke as he reclined at the table with his friends on that night. Jesus took some familiar foodstuffs – bread and wine – and blessed them in traditional Jewish fashion. But instead of going on to celebrate the inauguration of God's covenant with the people centuries before

PONTIUS PILATE

Pontius Pilate was the fifth Roman prefect of Judea, coming to power in AD 26 in succession to Valerius Gratus. He ruled for ten years. Little is known of him before he received this appointment, though legend has it that he was born at Fortingall, a remote spot in the highlands of Scotland which his father allegedly reached while serving with the legions on the northern edge of the empire. As procurator of Judea, Pilate's normal residence would be in Caesarea, and his name has been found there on an inscription, which confirms that he was known by the title of "prefect". Pilate was accompanied by his wife (Matthew 27:19), which was a relatively recent innovation introduced by the Roman senate only five years before his appointment.

Pilate's only claim to any sort of fame relates to his involvement in the death of Jesus. The Roman author Tacitus (*Annals* 15.44) only mentions him in this connection, though the Jewish writers Josephus and Philo both supply more information about his general disposition. They had a low opinion

of him, and describe him as a brutal and callous man who cared little either for Jewish religious scruples or for common human values. One passage in the gospels refers to an occasion when he ordered the death of certain Galileans , and "mingled their blood with their sacrifices" (Luke 13:1). This was probably the occasion described by Josephus, when Pilate had raided the temple treasury for cash to build an aqueduct, only to face demonstrations from crowds of outraged believers when he made a visit to Jerusalem, presumably for one of the festivals. In retaliation, Pilate sent his troops into the crowd in disguise, and a considerable number were killed while he himself sat and watched the gory spectacle (Josephus, *The Jewish War* 2.169-174). It could well be that this was why Antipas never had much time for Pilate (Luke 23:12), and it may have been sensitivity to this situation that led Pilate to send Jesus to him for trial.

Eventually, Pilate's cruelty and careless disregard for religious sensitivities led to him being summoned to Rome to give an

account of himself. What happened then is unknown. Some traditions claim that he and his wife later became Christians, and the Coptic church honours them both as saints and martyrs. But Eusebius reports more plausibly that he eventually committed suicide during the reign of Gaius (AD 37-41). His rule was the second longest of all the procurators, which suggests he may well have been an efficient administrator. But the gospels present him as a weak man, and an opportunist who condemned Jesus to death not out of any respect for the Jews, but only as a means of preserving his own reputation with the authorities back in Rome, who had already had to endure enough problems during his rule in Judea.

at Mount Sinai, he asserted that this meal itself would signal the beginning of a totally new chapter in God's dealings with the world. A new covenant would be inaugurated through his own impending death. The disciples would be familiar with some of the things Jesus said. The idea of a new covenant went back to the teaching of Jeremiah (Jeremiah 31:31), while the possibility that the death of a martyr would benefit others was not altogether new either. At the time of the Maccabean revolt, the death of innocent people had liberated Israel. But the solemnity of this occasion, and the words that Jesus used, all suggested that this was to be a crucial turning point in God's dealings with the human race. And when the earliest Christians later reflected on how it was all accomplished, they had no hesitation in seeing it in this light.

After the singing of a hymn (presumably one of the great Hallel Psalms, with which the Passover traditionally concluded), Jesus and the disciples went out to walk in the Garden of Gethsemane. The word Gethsemane means "oil press", and in ancient times there had probably been a large olive orchard there. Jesus often spent time in prayer at significant points in his life, and this was no exception. By a large rock which is now incorporated into the Franciscan Church of All Nations (built in 1924, but on the site of previous sanctuaries going back to the fourth century), Jesus poured out his deepest feelings as he faced up to the reality of what was about to happen. He expressed some powerful emotions, which reveal the apprehension that he felt at this time (Mark 14:32-6). But the disciples shared none of these feelings, and fell asleep until Judas arrived along with those who came to arrest Jesus. Almost before the others knew what was happening, Jesus had been carted off to the home of high priest Caiaphas, and was being officially interrogated. Peter followed, and maybe others did too (Mark 14:51-6). Almost certainly this was not a formal trial, but an informal enquiry by a small group of people, convened for the purpose of gathering evidence and making out a case against Jesus. In any case, it was only the Roman governor Pontius Pilate whose court had any legal standing in matters that might involve the death penalty.

Eventually, then, Jesus was brought to Pilate. Pilate's normal headquarters would be in Caesarea, but he travelled to Jerusalem for special occasions like Passover, when there was always a chance of some trouble. He probably stayed at Herod's old palace, and this was where Jesus met him, at what John calls "the pavement" (18:31). The earlier discussions at the high priest's residence centred on religious affairs. Was Jesus claiming to be the Messiah, and if so what did he mean by that? By all accounts, Jesus' response convinced the Jewish leaders that he was guilty of blasphemy – a grave charge that itself was punishable with death under Jewish law. But things of that sort were of no interest to Pilate, and when Jesus appeared before him he insisted that more acceptable charges be brought.

Three accusations were made (Luke 23:2): that Jesus misled the people; that he forbade paying taxes to Caesar (the usual charge against Zealots); and that he claimed to be a king (a title only the Roman senate could give). After interviewing Jesus, Pilate was uneasy with all this. Jesus may have upset Jewish sensitivities, but was he really guilty of any crime under

Bedouin children returning from a water hole in the Negev Desert.

Roman law? If he had claimed to be a king, he was obviously not the kind who could rob the emperor of his power. In terms of Roman law, Pilate might have been inclined to discharge Jesus. But upsetting the Jews was itself a serious thing, and if Pilate ignored the offence Jesus had apparently caused, it could easily spark off a riot – something that was guaranteed to make Pilate very unpopular back in Rome. According to Luke, he sent Jesus off to Herod Antipas (ruler of Galilee), who happened to be in Jerusalem – and who would be far more knowledgeable about the intricacies of Jewish politics. But Antipas was unwilling to take Pilate's decisions for him. So Pilate offered to release Jesus as a mark of goodwill, since it was Passover time. No such custom is documented anywhere else, but it would be a natural gesture for a governor to make at a time of national celebration. Even this backfired, however, when the crowd preferred a convicted murderer instead, a man named Barabbas.

The city walls of Jerusalem: the Golden Gate is to the right. In every account, Pilate appears as a weak man and an indecisive ruler. In reality, he was in

THE RESURRECTION

Belief that Jesus rose from the dead has always been central to the Christian faith. Wherever we look in the New Testament, the common conviction both of those who were his immediate disciples, and of their later converts, was that Jesus was no longer dead, but alive – continuing his work in and through the Christian communities that soon emerged in every significant town in the Roman empire. Many remarkable claims have been made about Jesus. But the idea that he rose from death is the most extraordinary feature of all the stories about him. And while many modern people find themselves attracted to his lifestyle and teaching, they are not at all sure what to think of Christian claims about the resurrection.

One recent view, for example, much popularised by the media, suggests that none of Jesus' original disciples ever thought of believing he had risen to life again. Belief in the resurrection was a late idea, it is claimed, only coming to prominence after the Christians had been forced to leave Jerusalem at the time of the Jewish revolt against the Romans (AD 66-70). Up until then, they regularly met for worship at the tomb of Jesus. But what could they do once they had been barred from entering the city? To answer that question, the story of the empty tomb was put together to explain why, after all, they did not need to worship there.

Worship at the tombs of heroes is a common practice. It happened in Jesus' day (see Matthew 23:29), and modern visitors to Israel can still join throngs of worshippers at the

tombs of Abraham in Hebron, of David in Jerusalem, and of some of the ancient rabbis as well. Nowadays, lines of Christian pilgrims also make their way to the Church of the Resurrection, and the Garden Tomb. But to suggest that the discontinuation of such a practice in the first century led to belief that Jesus was alive is completely far-fetched. For one thing, there is no evidence that anybody at all was interested in the place where Jesus was buried earlier than the fourth century. In addition, we have the statements made by Paul in 1 Corinthians, written at least ten years before AD 66. One gospel had certainly been written by then – probably more. And these accounts were undoubtedly based on stories that went right back into the earliest days of the church. It makes no sense at all to suppose that belief in the resurrection was a late development. The fact is that Christians did not venerate the tomb of Jesus because they believed there was nothing in it. And they held this belief right from the start.

But were they right? All the gospels say that three days after his burial Jesus' tomb was empty. But they do not all tell the same story. This may appear to be an argument against their reliability. It is actually a strong argument on the other side. Eye witnesses often give very different accounts of what they have seen, even when they are reporting everyday occurrences. Imagine how they might have coped with something as remarkable as a dead person coming to life again. The

disciples themselves no more expected such a thing to happen than you or I would. According to Mark 9:9-10, the very notion of "resurrection" was alien to their whole way of thinking. Is it surprising that they did not tell a logical and coherent story? If such an unbelievable story had been made up, we might reasonably expect they would have made sure that it at least sounded consistent. And what ancient writer would ever have invented a story in which the main witnesses were women – people who were generally given no credence at all as witnesses to anything? For all its variations, the evidence unequivocally points to the fact that Jesus' body disappeared from its tomb. The Jewish scholar, Geza Vermes, sums up the evidence in this way:

When every argument has been considered and weighed, the only conclusion acceptable to the historian must be ... that the women who set out to pay their last respects to Jesus found to their consternation, not a body, but an empty tomb.

So the question becomes, why was the tomb empty? The New Testament supplements the story of the empty tomb with a series of other stories in which the "risen" Jesus allegedly appeared to various people. What can we make of these? Perhaps these people were mistaken? They thought they were meeting their dead master, miraculously raised back to life. But at best they were having visions – at worst, perhaps, hallucinations. The ancient world knew of all these possibilities. Several Greek and

Bethphage. A tomb cut into the rock-face with a rolling stone across the entrance.

Egyptian cults claimed to be able to give their worshippers experiences in which deities such as Isis and Asclepius would appear to them. But such visions were not quite the same as what the Christians were claiming. These were mythical figures from the long forgotten past, so nobody really knew what they looked like anyway. But Jesus was well-known to the disciples. He had died not long before. They would know if it was him alright. In addition, his appearances just happened, whereas these other alleged visions of gods and goddesses were produced to order by the use of various well-tried hypnotic rituals.

Several facts make it unlikely that the disciples were the victims of some sort of psychological trick. We may discount any possibility that grave robbers had stolen Jesus' body: such people would only be interested in the rich and famous, not in someone who died in penury as a common criminal. If Jesus' tomb was empty, only three groups of people could have removed his body: the Jews, the Romans, or the disciples themselves. Jews and Romans both had a vested interest in squashing the Christian message. They could have done so by producing a body, if they had one.

Since they did not, we may presume that they had not taken it. So what about the disciples? They were prepared to stake their lives on the fact that Jesus was alive. Many of them were brutally murdered for their faith, including Peter and other members of Jesus' inner circle, who would be prime suspects for removing the body. It is simply impossible to believe they would willingly suffer in this way if all the time they knew where they themselves had hidden Jesus' body.

Nor is there any evidence that the resurrection appearances were hallucinatory experiences. Paul's understanding is of special value here, for unlike the other disciples he was psychically experienced. He writes of having had visions and revelations of a mystical nature on several occasions (2 Corinthians 12:1-6). But he was quite sure that meeting with the risen Jesus was a completely different sort of experience. It was not visionary – but neither was it quite the same as meeting Jesus before the crucifixion had been. Though the New

Testament everywhere stresses the recognisable continuity between Jesus of Nazareth and the risen Christ, Jesus' risen body was more than just a return to what had been before. He appeared and disappeared in rooms with closed doors. And even those who knew him quite well – Mary Magdalene, the couple on the road to Emmaus, the disciples in a boat on Galilee – failed to recognise the risen Jesus, even though they had seen him only a few days before. His physical appearance had obviously changed in some way.

So what did it all mean? The New Testament makes three claims about the resurrection. On the day of Pentecost, Peter declared that the resurrection was clear proof that "God has made this Jesus, whom you crucified, both Lord and Messiah" (Acts 2:36). Because of the resurrection, Jesus' disciples knew for certain that his claims to a unique relationship with God were actually true. But they also believed that Jesus' resurrection gave believers in Christ a direct personal access to God's own power. The power that raised Jesus from death was now available to ordinary people, to empower and equip them to live a satisfying life. Because Jesus had opposed the forces of evil, and won, his followers could have the power to do the same. The Holy Spirit, or the Spirit of Christ, as Paul sometimes called it. Then, finally, the resurrected Jesus was described as "the first fruits of those who have fallen asleep" (1 Cor 15:20). The fact that Jesus rose from death is a sign and promise that his followers too will survive death.

the Roman empire, but they were even prepared to die for their belief that it was true. Over the centuries, the exact significance of belief in the resurrection has been debated and explained in many different ways. But it still stands at the centre of Christian faith, and what follows it in the New Testament only serves to underline yet further the unique significance of Jesus.

ASCENSION AND GLORY

The ascension as such features only in Luke's story of Jesus' life. It is unclear whether Luke 24:50-53 tells of it, for in some ancient manuscripts the crucial words "and was taken up into heaven" are missing. But Luke certainly documents it in more detail in Acts 1:6-11. This story really marks the point at which the regular resurrection appearances of Jesus ceased. As such, it is merely the culmination of several occasions when Jesus had disappeared from his disciples' gaze in the forty days following the resurrection. From the time of the resurrection itself, Jesus had been exalted into the presence of God. When he left the couple at Emmaus, he did not return to some kind of earth-bound limbo, but to the heavenly glory into which, as the risen Son of Man, he had now entered. The actual story of the ascension presumably marks some special occasion when he left the disciples in a dramatic and memorable way – and after which, they saw him no more. Though the ascension story itself is only recorded by Luke, the idea is referred to in several passages in John (20:17, 13:1, 16:10, 17:11), while Matthew concludes with the conviction that Jesus has received precisely the kind of universal authority that the ascension story seems to imply.

Modern western people sometimes have difficulty with the notion that Jesus was taken "up into heaven". Certainly, we no longer share the perception of ancient people, that the universe was a kind of three-tiered construction, with the earth sandwiched in the middle between heaven and hell. In this frame of reference, it would be natural to think of Jesus being taken "up to heaven". But even today, that could easily be a natural, commonsense way to describe such a disappearance. Acts 1:12 seems to place the ascension on the Mount of Olives, and Constantine subsequently built a church around a cave that he believed marked the spot. Later tradition identified an open space as the more likely site of the ascension. In 384 AD, Egeria joined in a celebration of the ascension on a small hill a little further up the Mount of Olives, and some six years later a pilgrim called Poemenia had a shrine constructed there – around a rock which bears a mark allegedly made by Jesus' right foot as he said farewell to his disciples.

The New Testament's concern is not with such spatial distinctions, but with the fact that Jesus himself had returned to be exalted in glory with God. This was always implicit in the title "Son of Man" applied to Jesus, for in the Old Testament book of Daniel this character received "authority, honour and royal power" (Daniel 7:14). Not long after the event, the cross itself was seen as Christ's final battle with the forces of evil, and his resurrection as the proof that he had triumphed. The ascension demonstrated that this victory was absolute. In the words of Rudolf Bultmann, a great New Testament scholar of a previous generation, "Christ's ascent to heaven is ... the act of subjugating the demonic world rulers ... hence the whole cosmos ... – heavenly, earth, subterranean beings – must pay homage to the exalted Lord ... God has appointed an end for the cosmic disorder which originated in the primaeval fall, and through [Christ], has reconciled all things to himself ..."

THE REST OF THE STORY

In the opening words of his gospel, Mark claimed that what he was describing was only "the beginning of the good news of Jesus Christ". By the time he was writing, in the mid-60s of the first century, he knew that the rest of the story was at least as exciting. For though Jesus' life, death and resurrection were central, what happened afterwards was every bit as remarkable as that 33-year life in Galilee and Judea. During that period, Jesus had been only a local hero. He never travelled beyond the land of his birth, nor did he attract the rich and famous to follow him. But within less than a generation, his name was known in every major city around the Mediterranean Sea, and his followers were growing in numbers and influence almost daily. Women and men who began life in the remote villages of rural Galilee suddenly found new power and direction in their lives, as they were thrust on to the centre of the world stage to speak of their undying love for this remarkable person from Galilee.

By this stage, of course, they were quite certain that Jesus was more than just a human being. Peter was the one who made the first faltering moves towards believing that Jesus was the Messiah, on that remarkable occasion at Caesarea Philippi which forms the watershed of Mark's story (Mark 8:27-30). But within a matter of months, Peter and the others were confidently claiming not only that Jesus was the Messiah – albeit a rather different kind of Messiah from the one commonly anticipated – but they were also asserting that he was "the Lord". In the Roman world, the title Lord was one of the special honours accorded to the emperor, and by applying it to Jesus his followers were affirming their own loyalty to his person and message. But in the Jewish world, the very same word had been set apart for an even more

An ancient stepped street in Jerusalem with the Mount of Olives in the distance.

Through history followers of Jesus have been motivated by their Christian faith to effect change in society, often at great personal cost. William Wilberforce, Dietrich Bonhoeffer, Martin Luther King and Bishop Desmond Tutu are just four of many millions of social reformers.

exalted use. In the Greek translation of the Old Testament that was used by the early church (as well as Jews throughout the empire), the word "lord" translated the personal name of God. There can be no doubt that the earliest Christians soon came to recognise Jesus himself as God, and that this belief can be traced right back to the earliest days of the church in Jerusalem. Writing to the predominantly Gentile congregation in Corinth, Paul was later to quote a saying that had been handed on in Aramaic from the first generation of disciples: *Maranatha*, which means "may our Lord come" (1 Corinthians 16:22).

Belief in Jesus as Messiah and Lord quickly spread throughout the first century world. What began as a small and persecuted minority faith was embraced by the emperor Constantine (AD 280-337), and as a result of his conversion Christianity became the dominant faith of the Roman empire. Over the last 2000 years, people in every generation and in all countries have been attracted by the figure of Jesus of Nazareth. Christians have often misunderstood his teachings. The church has frequently displayed the very same social and religious attitudes that Jesus so strongly opposed. But Jesus Christ has lost none of his attractiveness. Today there are more than 2 billion Christians in the world, and the figure is growing every day. Westerners will find this hard to

comprehend, for this growth is taking place largely in the countries of the developing world, where people of all sorts are discovering that Jesus meets their needs. But as the focus of world trade and civilisation shifts away from the west, so Christianity is now no longer predominantly a western faith. Its roots were in an ancient oriental culture (Jesus was not a white man), and today the majority of the world's Christians are non-white and non-western.

Throughout history, Jesus' followers have been at the forefront of social reform and political innovation. Lord Shaftesbury was a nineteenth-century English aristocrat, who affirmed the rights of women and children in a culture that was abusing them as if they were animals. William Wilberforce, his older contemporary, was instrumental in securing the abolition of the slave trade. In the mid-twentieth century, Dietrich Bonhoeffer opposed the Nazi war machine – and died for it. Martin Luther King gave African Americans the courage to exercise their civil rights, and paid the price with his own life. Desmond Tutu withstood pressure and intimidation to affirm the right of his own race to self-determination. All these, and many more unsung heroes, were motivated by their Christian faith and their deep love for Jesus. All over the world today, Jesus' followers are making a difference. The message of this remarkable person still speaks across the centuries, and gives hope to today's marginalised people, and challenge to the well-off. As Clement of Alexandria, an ancient church leader, once put it, "The Lord has turned all our sunsets into sunrise."

The reason for this is not hard to find. It is not just that Jesus' teachings enshrine noble truths – though they do. Nor is it merely that he was such an attractive personality – though he was. It is in the discovery that the living Christ can empower ordinary people in a way that gives new meaning and purpose to life. Before his crucifixion, Jesus made a remarkable promise to the disciples: "the one who believes in me will also do the works that I do and, in fact, will do greater works than these, because I am going to the Father" (John 14:12). The continuing availability of the power of the Holy Spirit was the key to these "greater works". The Spirit played a major role in Jesus' own life and ministry, commissioning him at his baptism, and inspiring and guiding him subsequently. It was the same Spirit whom he imparted to his disciples after the resurrection (John 20:22). The remarkable events of the Day of Pentecost (Acts 2:1-47) merely highlighted what the disciples already knew to be true: that the Spirit of Christ would always be with them, to help them be like Jesus, and to equip them for the task to which he called them. That presence and that task have spanned the centuries, and still move and motivate those who reflect on the meaning of Jesus in today's very different world.

Index